W9-BKU-113

Early Learning Basic Skills

by
Sherrill B. Flora

illustrated by
Julie Anderson

Publisher
Key Education Publishing Company, LLC
Minneapolis, Minnesota

CONGRATULATIONS ON YOUR PURCHASE OF A KEY EDUCATION PRODUCT!

The editors at Key Education are former teachers who bring experience, enthusiasm, and quality to each and every product. Thousands of teachers look to the staff at Key Education for new and innovative resources to make their work more enjoyable and rewarding. Key Education is committed to developing educational materials that will assist teachers in building a strong and developmentally appropriate curriculum for young children.

PLAN FOR GREAT TEACHING EXPERIENCES WHEN YOU USE EDUCATIONAL MATERIALS FROM KEY EDUCATION PUBLISHING COMPANY, LLC.

Credits
Author: Sherrill B. Flora
Inside Illustrations: Julie Anderson
Cover Design: Mary Claire
Editors: Kelly Huxmann
George C. Flora
Cover Photography: © Corbis

Key Education welcomes manuscripts and product ideas from teachers.
For a copy of our submission guidelines, please send a self-addressed, stamped envelope to:
Key Education Publishing Company, LLC
Acquisitions Department
9601 Newton Avenue South
Minneapolis, Minnesota 55431

ISBN: 1-933052-08-2
Early Learning Basic Skills
Copyright © 2005 by Key Education Publishing Company, LLC
Minneapolis, Minnesota 55431

Contents

Introduction

Early Learning Basic Skills provides early childhood teachers with everything they need to help develop and build a solid educational foundation for young learners. This resource offers a wealth of easy-to-use materials covering important topics and curriculum areas, such as beginning the school year, the alphabet, numbers, colors, shapes, fine motor skills, and basic concepts. Teachers will soon discover that the activities in *Early Learning Basic Skills* were designed not only to teach, but also to delight and motivate young children to want to learn.

This book includes over 150 reproducible pages that will engage young learners. These activities may be used in an instructional setting to reinforce a concept. They can also be offered as independent free-time activities or used as meaningful take-home projects that parents and children can complete together.

Early Learning Basic Skills will quickly become one of an early childhood teacher's most-valued educational resources!

Topics Covered Include:
- Beginning the School Year
- All About Me
- Pencil and Scissor Skills
- Colors and Shapes
- Basic Concepts
- Alphabet
- Beginning Consonant Sounds
- Handwriting
- 71 Sight Word Cards
- Numbers 0 to 30
- Measurement
- Numeral and Operational Symbols Flash Cards

PLUS — Fun Extras!
- My Own Color Book
- My Own Alphabet Book

Going to School

Fill in the blanks. Cut along the dotted line and glue to the inside of a paper plate. Punch a hole in the plate and string a piece of yarn through the hole so the paper plate can be worn as a necklace.

My name is:

_____.

I go to _____ school.

My teacher's name is

_____.

My phone number is:

_____.

All About Me

Have the children take this home and fill out the information with the help of their parents. Each child will use this as a "share and tell" experience.

My name is:	This is a picture of ME!
_____ I am _____ years old. I have _____ hair. I have _____ eyes. I am good at _____ .	
This is a picture of my family!	**This is my favorite thing!**

Draw a self-portrait and print your name.

This Is ME!

School Tools in My Backpack

Color, cut out, and glue the school tools on the backpack.
What do you think you will need?

glue

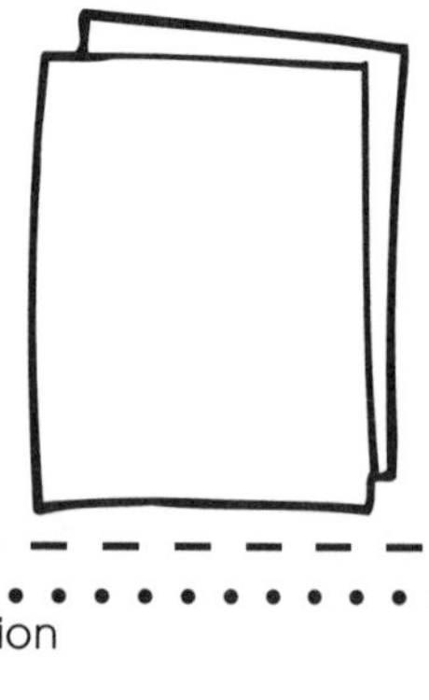

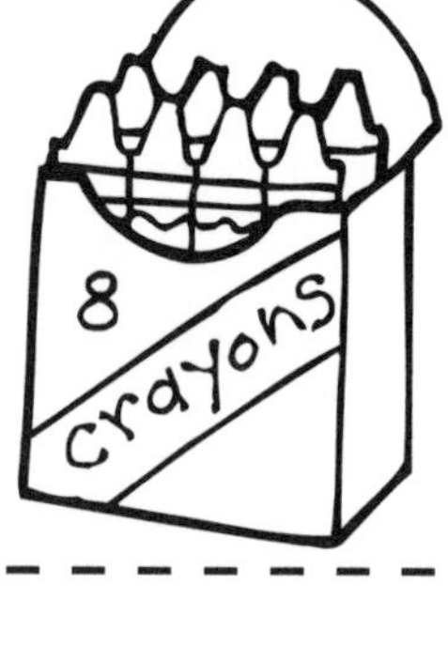

8 crayons

What Should I Eat?

Color, cut out, and glue the foods you would like to eat for lunch on the lunch bag.

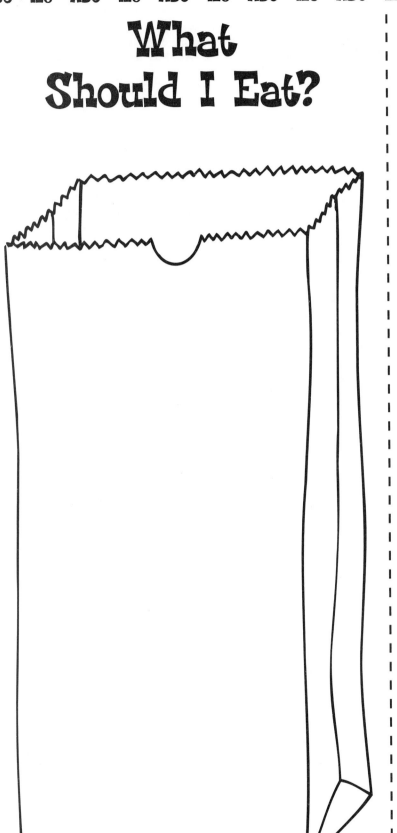

Riding the School Bus

Help the school bus find its way to school.

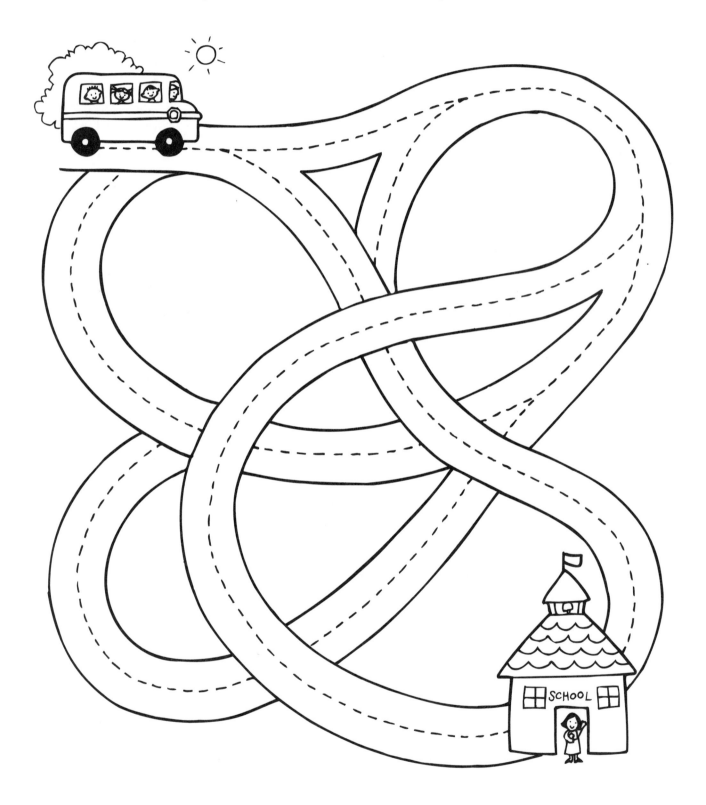

SCHOOL

Silly Squirrel

Color and cut out the squirrel and its tail. Attach the tail with a brass fastener.

Finished squirrel

Pumpkin Face

Color the pumpkin.
Cut out the eyes, mouth, and nose.
Glue on the pumpkin.

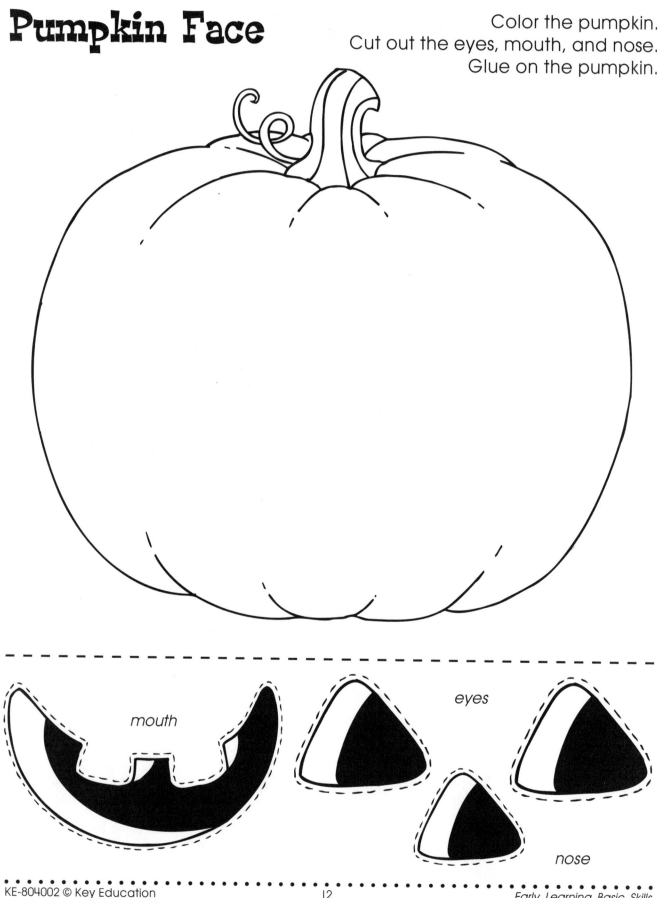

mouth

eyes

nose

Trace the Turkey's Feathers

Trace and color the turkey's feathers.

Matching Mittens

Draw lines to connect the matching mittens.

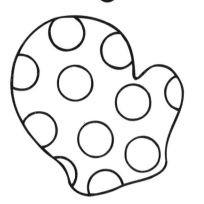

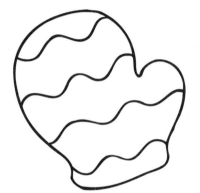

Snowman Puzzle

Cut out the pieces.
Glue or paste onto a large sheet of paper. Draw a face.

Finished snowman

Name_____

A Special Valentine

Color and cut out along the dotted lines. Fold and give to a special person.

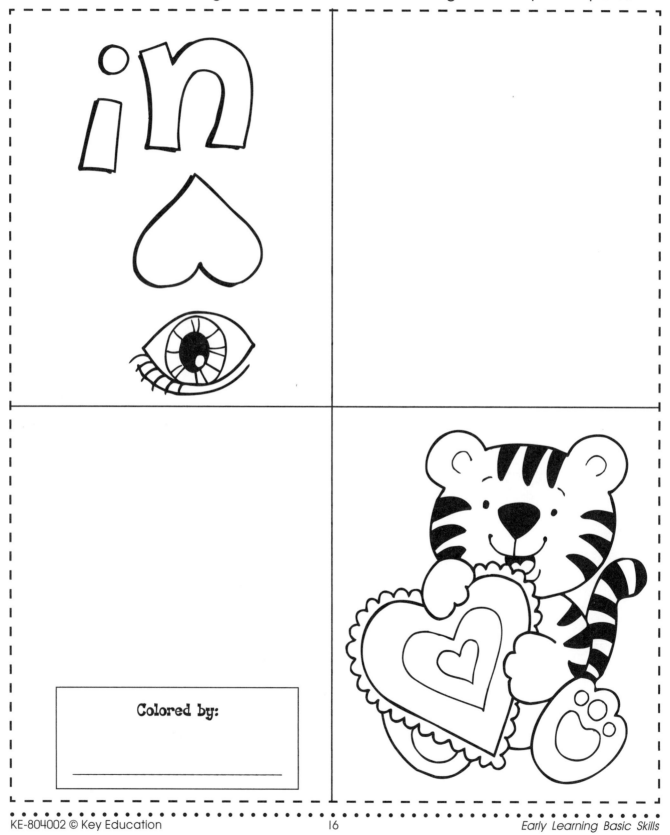

Colored by:

_____

Lion and Lamb Puppets

Color and cut out along the dotted lines. Tape to craft sticks and use as stick puppets.

Let's Go Fly a Kite!

Connect the dots and color.

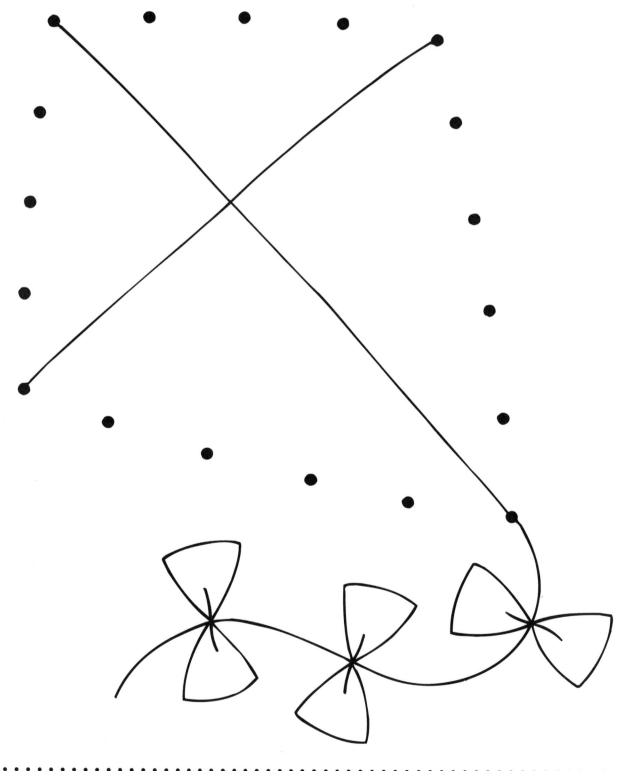

Umbrella Lacing Card

Copy onto heavy card stock. Color and cut out along the dotted lines. Punch holes and lace with yarn. To create a needle, wrap one end of the yarn with masking tape.

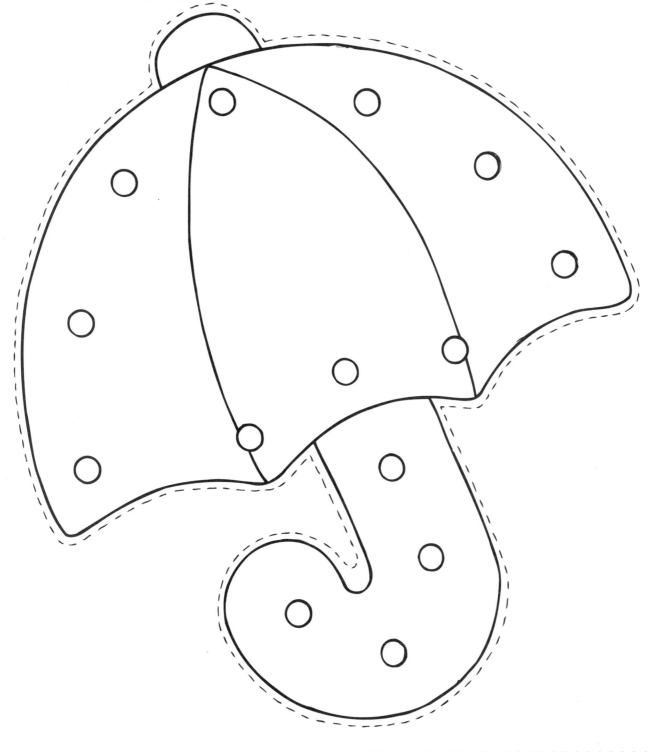

Fun At The Beach

Circle the things you would not find at the beach.

Summer Bugs!

Color and cut out along the dotted lines.
Glue together to create some crazy summer bugs!

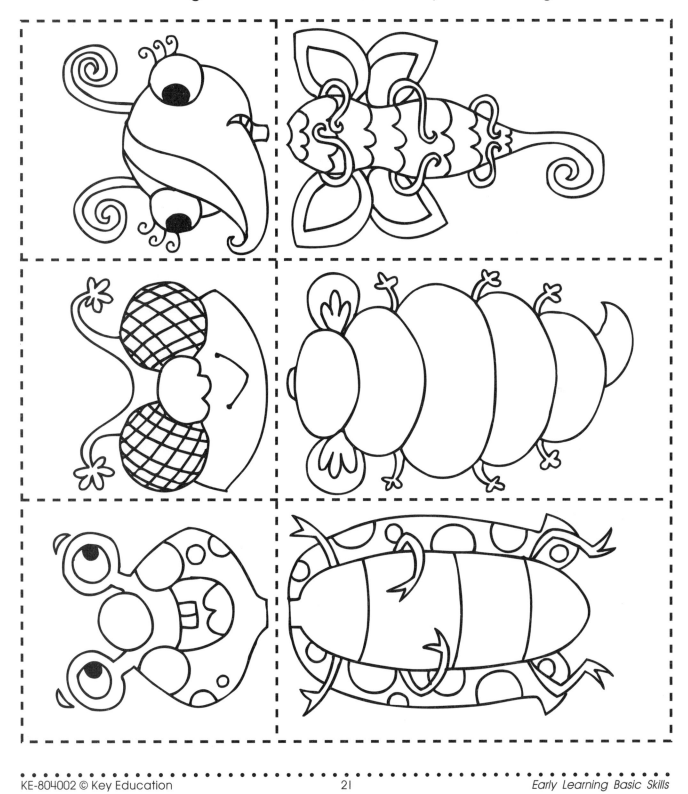

Sunflowers

Cut out the flowers and glue "crunched" yellow tissue paper on each petal.
Tape a straw to the back of each flower and place in a vase.

Down We Go!

Use your pencil to help the firefighters down the poles.

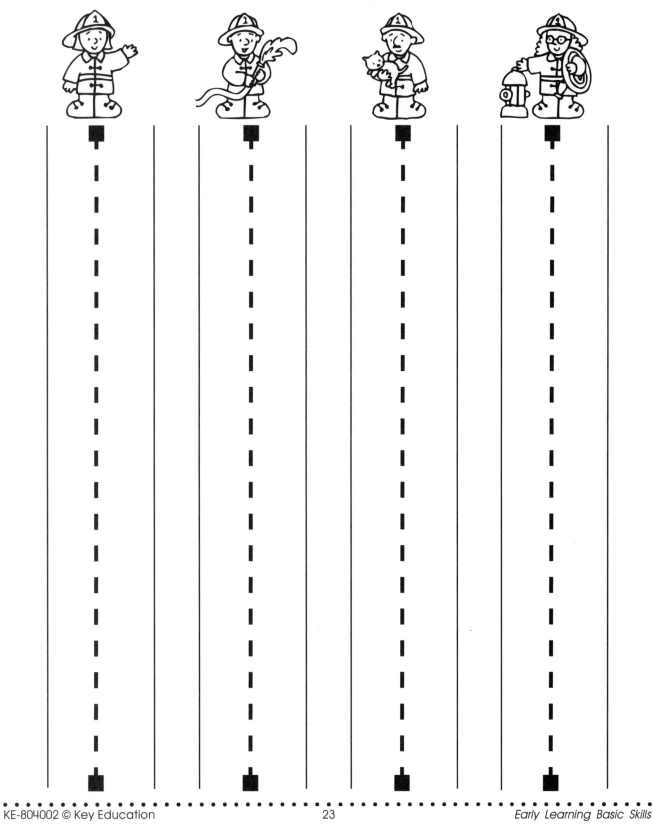

Down the Beanstalk

Use your pencil to help the characters down the beanstalks.

What a Web!

Use your pencil to help the spiders come down from their webs.

Down Came the Rain

Use your pencil to help the raindrops fall to the earth.

Feed the Furry Friends

Use your pencil to help the animals find their food.

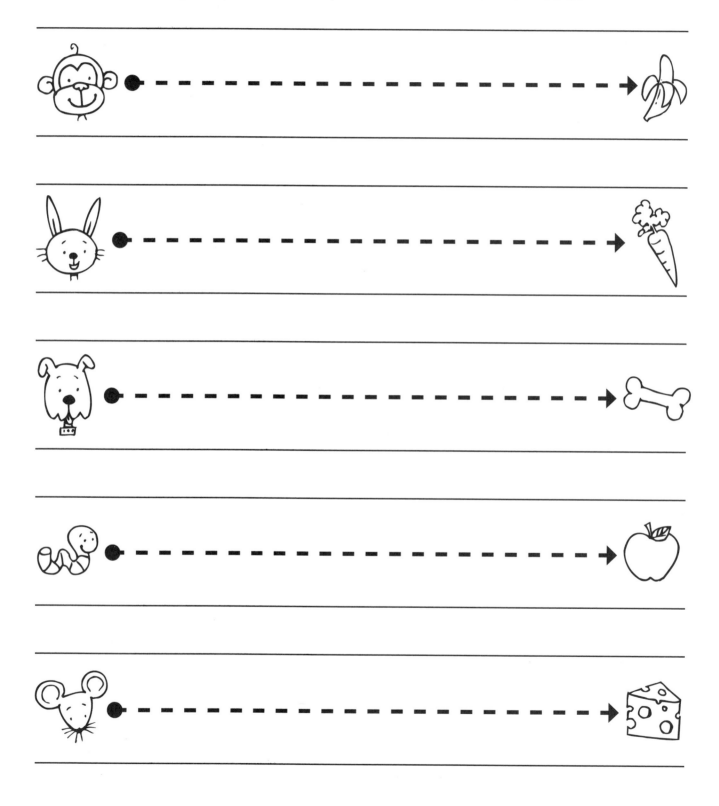

Where Is My Home?

Use your pencil to help the animals find their homes.

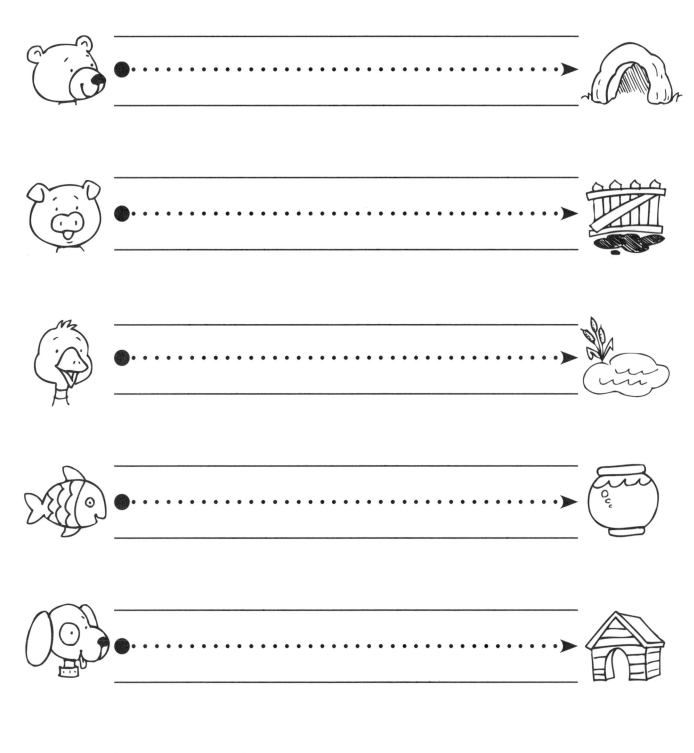

Ladybugs, Go Home!

Use your pencil to help the ladybugs get home.

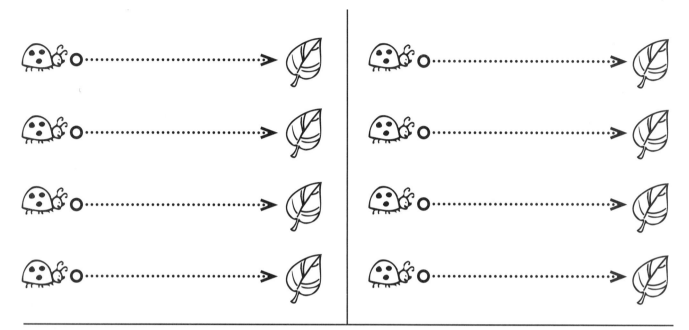

The Ants Are Invited to a Picnic!

Use your pencil to help the ant find the picnic food.

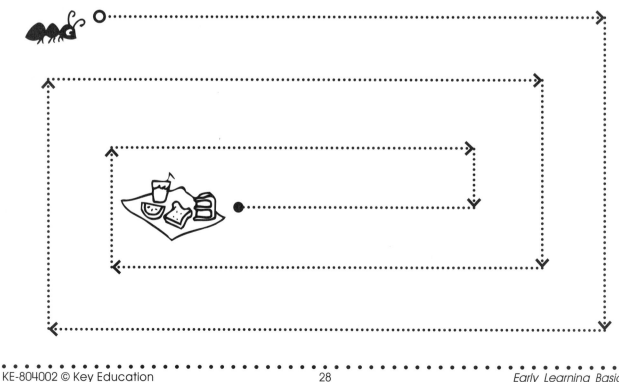

Little Birds, Fly Home!

Use your pencil to help the birds fly home.

Going in Circles!

Trace around the circles.

Silly Faces

Use your pencil to trace the circle around each face.

Follow the Path

Use your pencil to help the snake follow the path.

Cars on the Road

Use your pencil to trace the wheels on each vehicle. Color.

Race Around the Track!

Use your pencil to help the race car around the track.

Sliding Penguins

Use your pencil to help the penguins slide down the slopes.

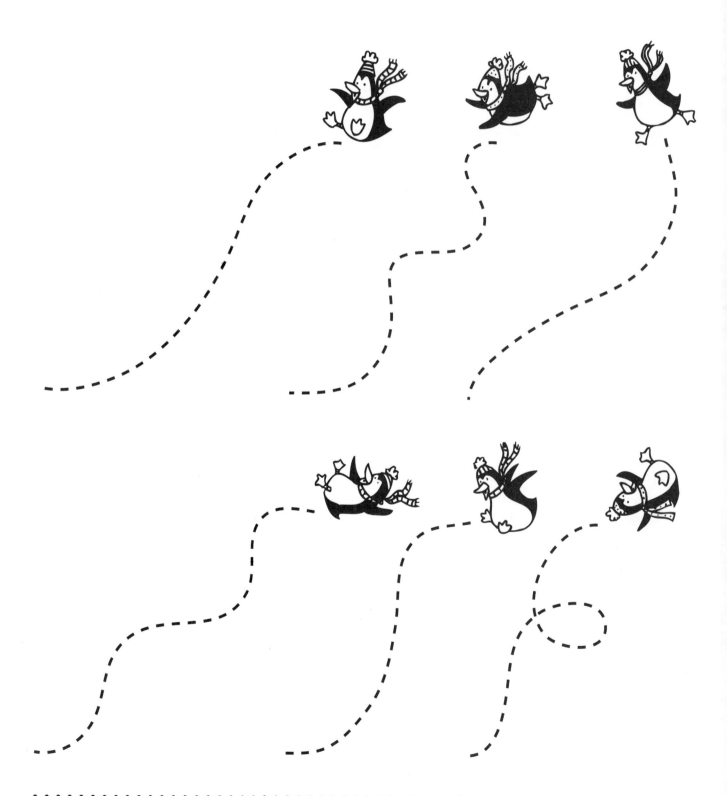

Sliding at the Park

Use your pencil to help the children go down the slides.

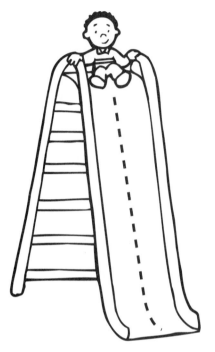

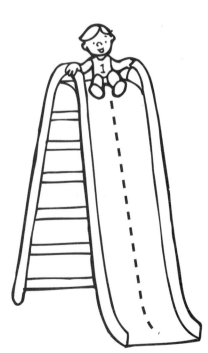
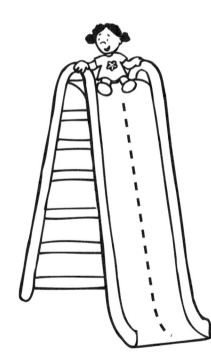
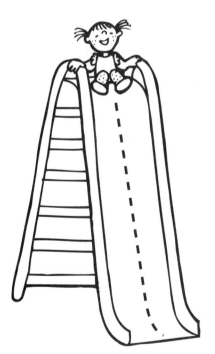

Fluttering Butterflies

Use your pencil to help the butterflies fly.

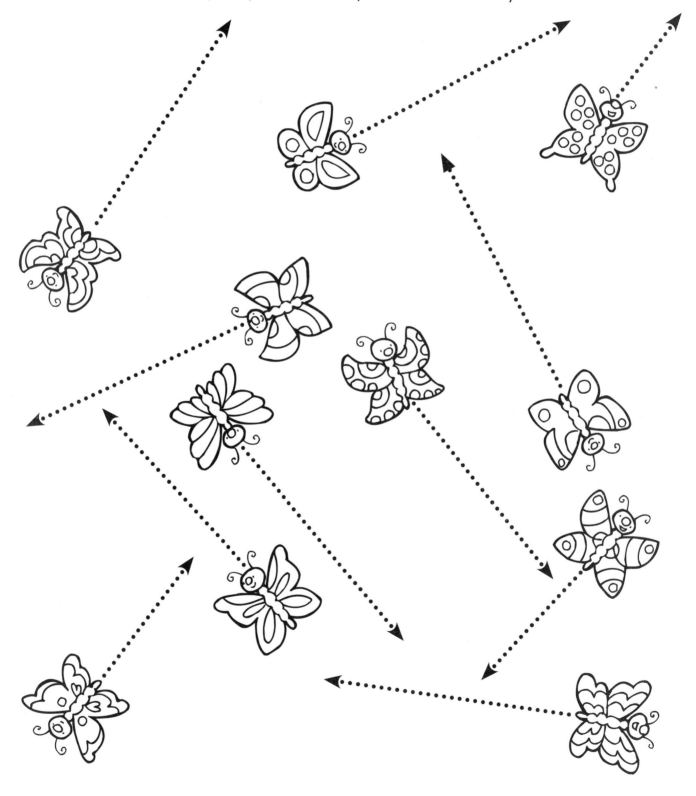

Circles

Trace the circles.

Color the circles.

Squares

Trace the squares.   Color the squares.

Circles and Squares

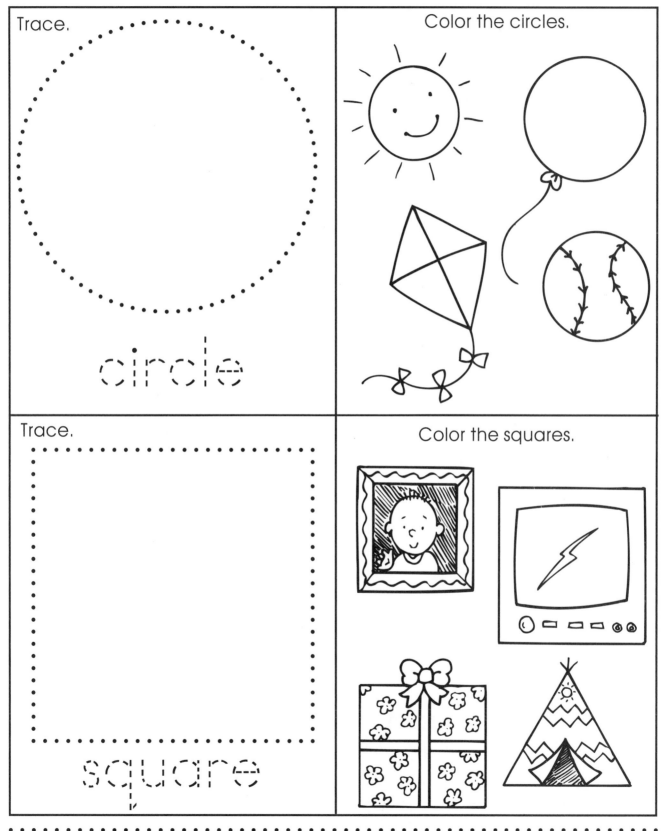

Trace.

circle

Color the circles.

Trace.

square

Color the squares.

Triangles

Trace the triangles.   Color the triangles.

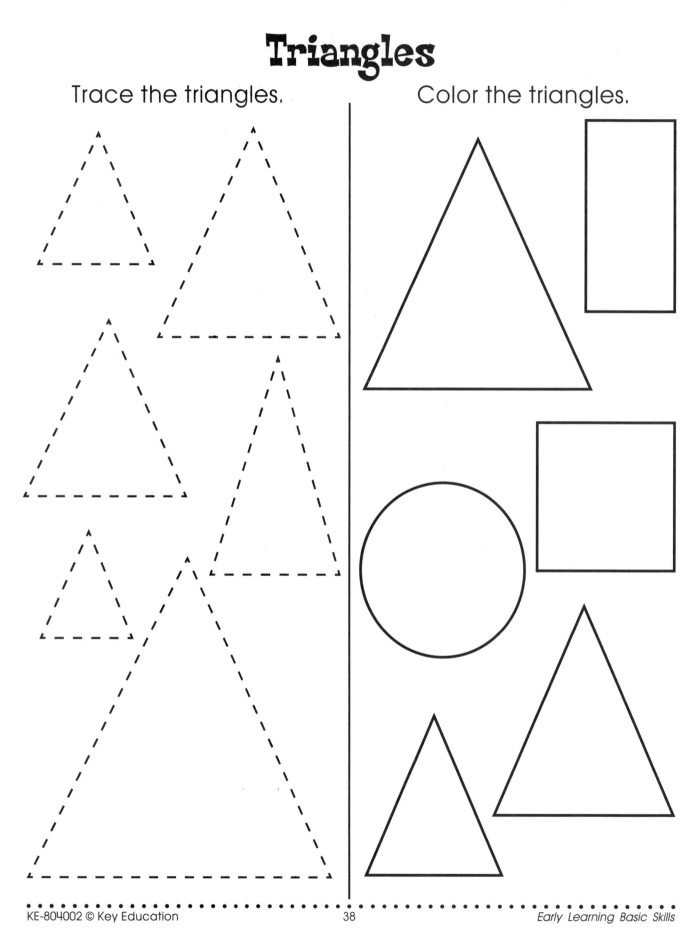

Rectangles

Trace the rectangles.   Color the rectangles.

Triangles and Rectangles

Trace.

triangle

Color the triangles.

Trace.

rectangle

Color the rectangles.

Diamonds

Trace the diamonds.   Color the diamonds.

Stars

Trace the stars.

Color the stars.

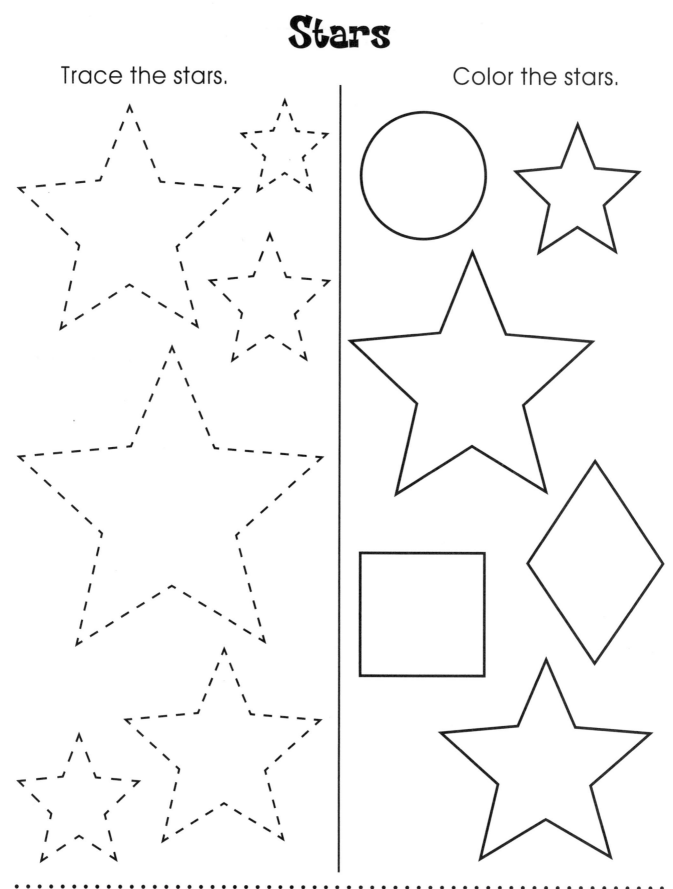

Stars and Diamonds

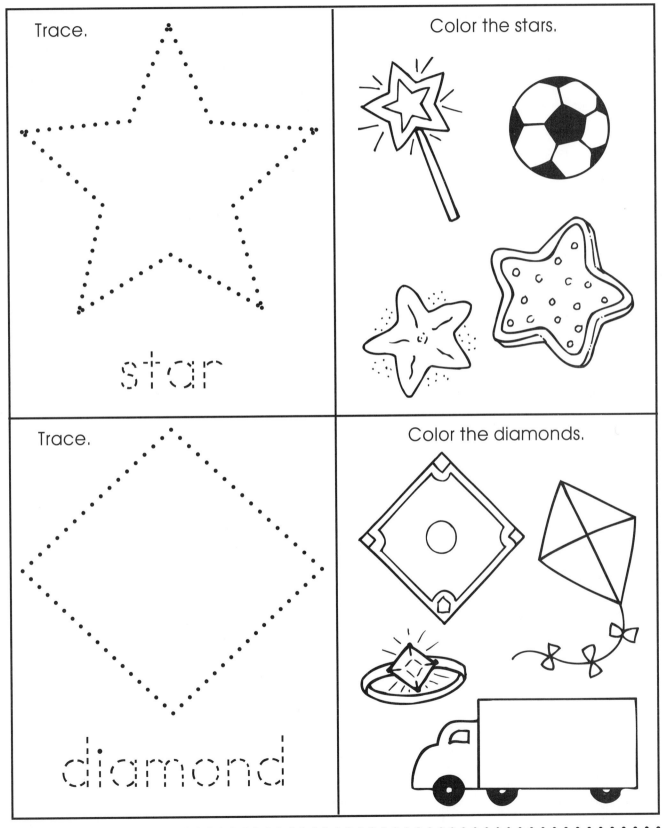

Trace.

star

Color the stars.

Trace.

diamond

Color the diamonds.

Ovals

Trace the ovals.   Color the ovals.

Octagons

Trace the octagons.   Color the octagons.

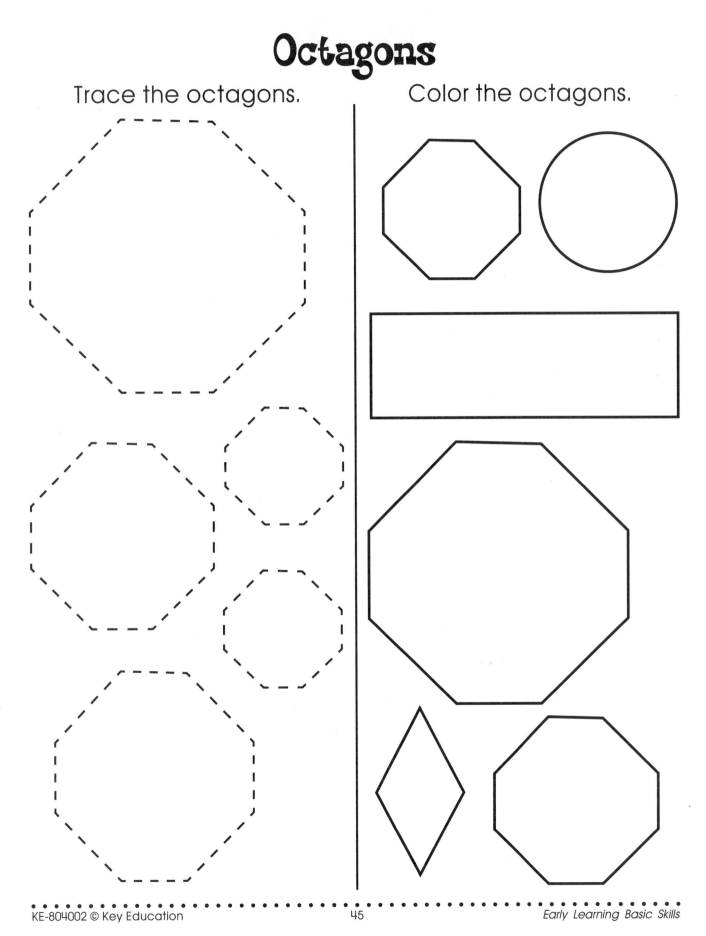

Ovals and Octagons

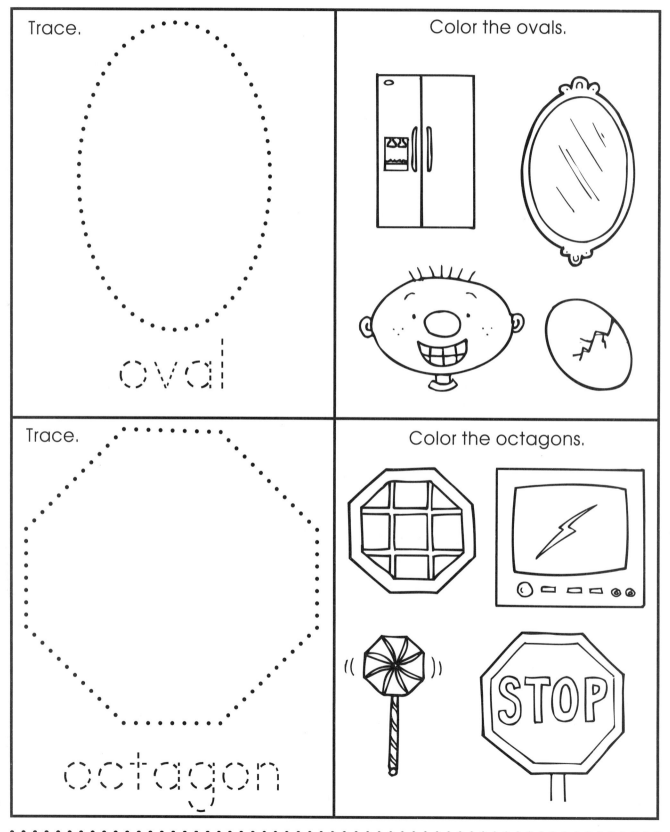

Trace.

oval

Color the ovals.

Trace.

octagon

Color the octagons.

Finish the Shapes

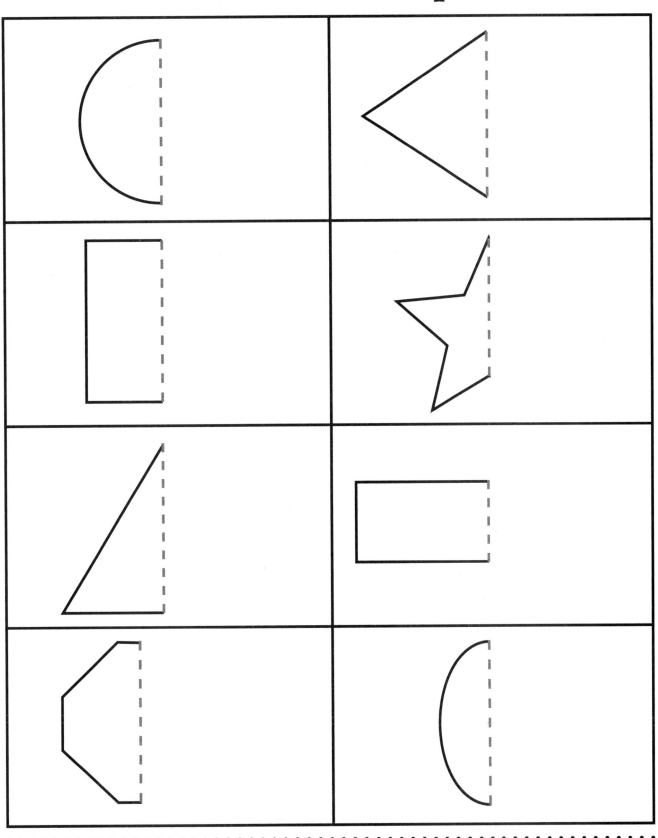

Match the Shapes!

Draw lines to match the shapes that are the same. Color.

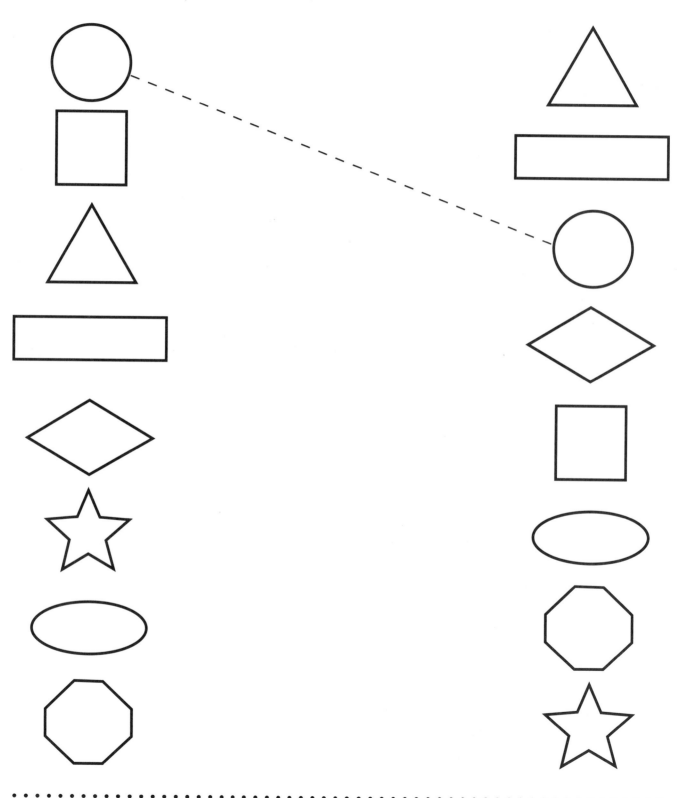

Color all the shapes that are the SAME!

Print.

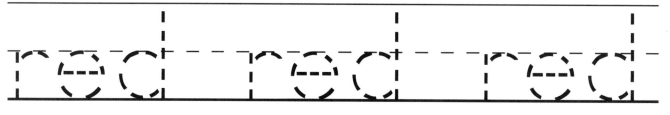

Color the apple **red**.

red

Circle the words that spell "**red**."

red	bed	sad	red	rid
and	red	red	rod	red

Name _____

Colors

ABC • **123** • **ABC** • **123** • **ABC** • **123** • **ABC** • **123** • **ABC** • **123** • **ABC** • **123** • **ABC** • **123** • **ABC**

Print.

blue blue blue

Color the bird **blue**.

blue

Circle the words that spell "**blue**."

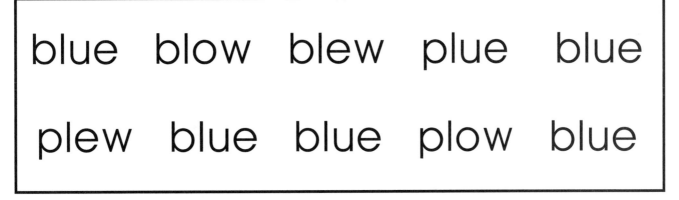

blue   blow   blew   plue   blue

plew   blue   blue   plow   blue

Print.

yellow   yellow

Color the sun **yellow**.

yellow

Circle the words that spell "**yellow**."

yollow	yellow	yellow	yullou
yellow	yullum	yellow	yallow

Flying High with Colors

Color the picture. Use red, blue, and yellow crayons.

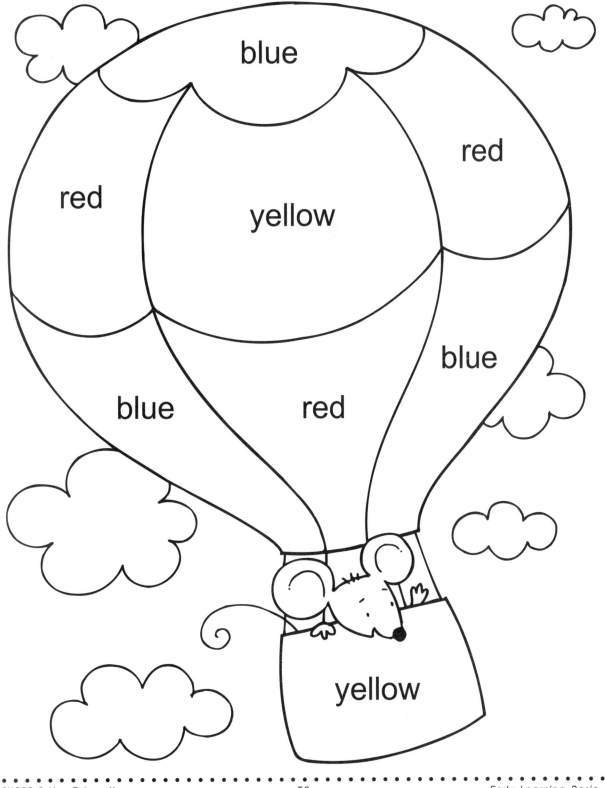

Print.

green   green

Color the frog **green**.

green

Circle the words that spell "**green**."

grean   green   green   green

green   grean   green   preen

Name _____

ABC • 123 • ABC • 123 • ABC • 123 • ABC • 123 • ABC • 123 • ABC • 123 • ABC • 123 • ABC

Print.

_____

orange orange

Color the pumpkin **orange**.

orange

Circle the words that spell "**orange**."

urange   orange   arange   orange

orange   orange   urange   orange

Print.

purple   purple

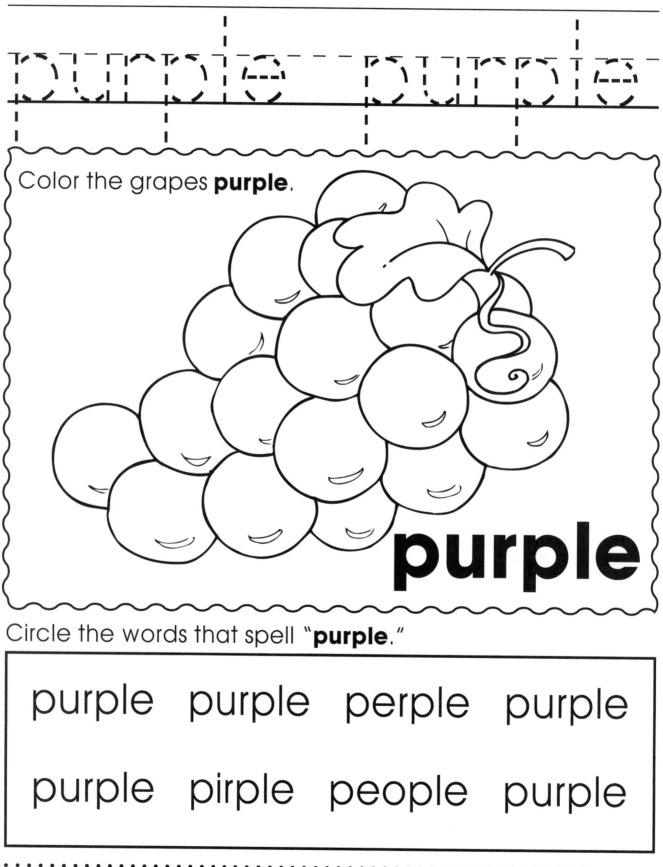

Color the grapes **purple**.

purple

Circle the words that spell "**purple**."

purple	purple	perple	purple
purple	pirple	people	purple

Butterfly Fun

Read the color words. Color the butterflies.

Print.

brown   brown

Color the puppy **brown**.

brown

Circle the words that spell "**brown**."

brown	brown	brown	broom
brown	bruun	brown	prown

Name _____

ABC • 123 • ABC • 123 • ABC • 123 • ABC • 123 • ABC • 123 • ABC • 123 • ABC • 123 • ABC

Print.

black   black

Color the cat **black**.

black

Circle the words that spell "**black**."

blaak	black	black	blaek
black	black	dlack	black

Hidden Picture Surprise!

Read the color words. Color the picture.

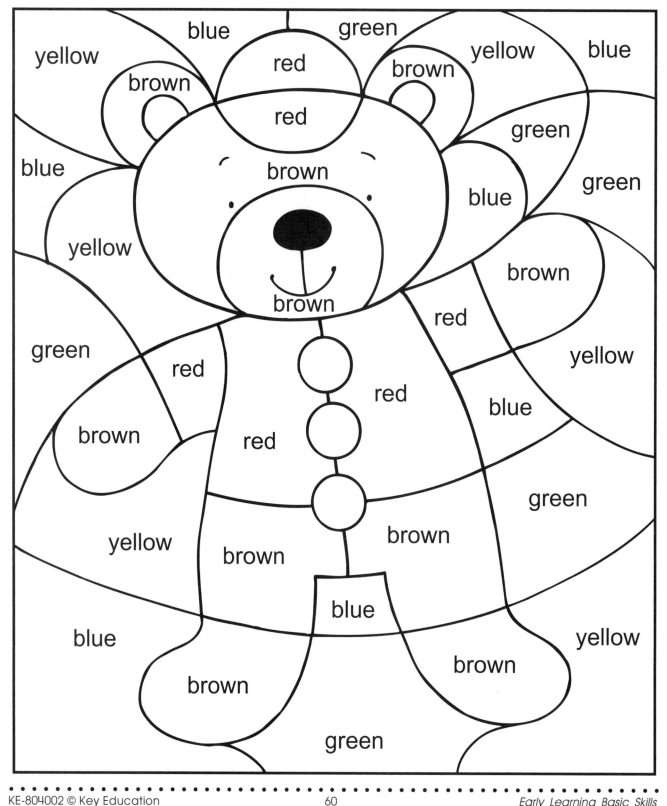

Print.

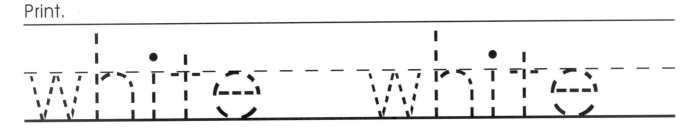

Color the bunny **white**.

white

Circle the words that spell "**white**."

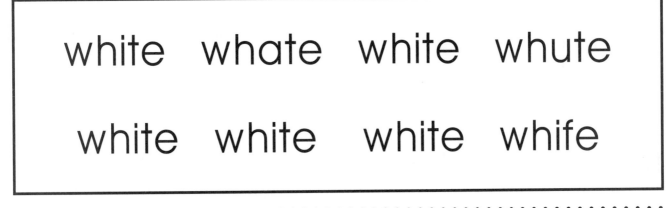

| white | whate | white | whute |
| white | white | white | whife |

Print.

pink pink pink

Color the flamingo **pink**.

pink

Circle the words that spell "**pink**."

pink	punk	pink	qink	pink
pink	pink	bink	pnik	pink

Clowning Around

Color the clown and his balloons.

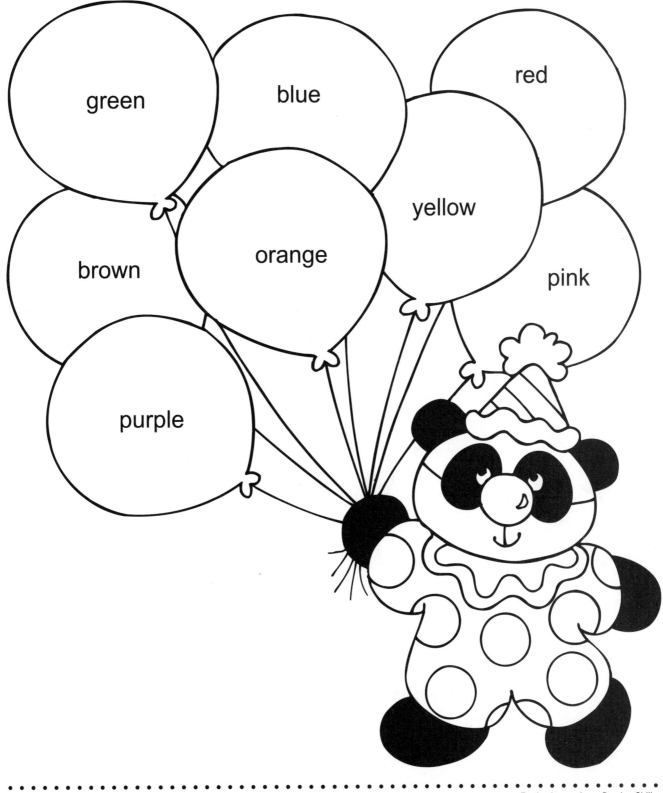

green

blue

red

brown

orange

yellow

pink

purple

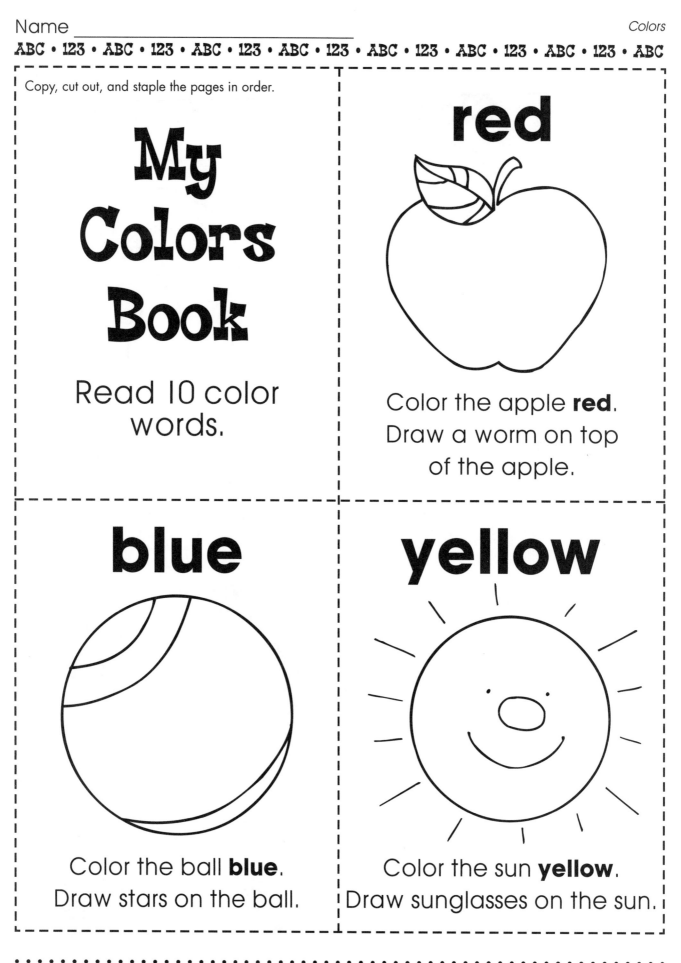

Copy, cut out, and staple the pages in order.

My Colors Book

Read 10 color words.

red

Color the apple **red**. Draw a worm on top of the apple.

blue

Color the ball **blue**. Draw stars on the ball.

yellow

Color the sun **yellow**. Draw sunglasses on the sun.

orange

Color the pumpkin **orange**.
Draw a face
on the pumpkin.

green

Color the frog **green**.
Draw a lily pad
under the frog.

purple

Color the grapes **purple**.
Draw a bowl
for the grapes.

pink

Color the flamingo **pink**.
Draw a pond
for the flamingo.

brown

Color the bear **brown**.
Draw a hat
on the bear's head.

black

Color the seal **black**.
Draw a ball
on the seal's nose.

white

Color the rabbit **white**.
Draw a basket.

My favorite color is

_____.

Draw a picture.

Rhyming Pairs

Color and cut out the pictures. Glue each picture next to the picture whose names rhyme.

Two-Piece Opposites Puzzles

Copy the puzzles onto card stock, color, and cut out.

Go-Togethers

Draw lines to connect the things that "go together."

Same/Different

Color the things that are the same in each row.

Bead Patterns

Look at the beads. Color the bead that should come next.

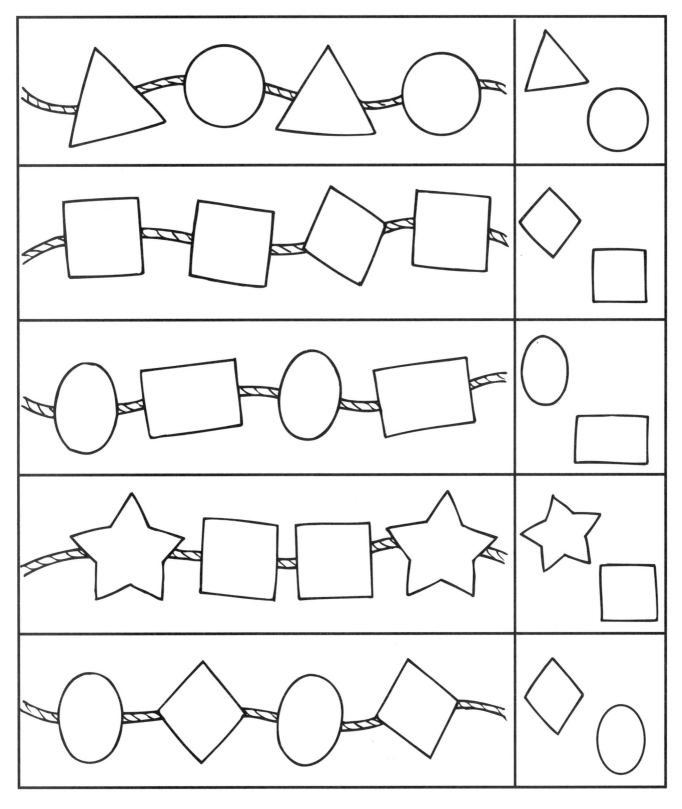

Sequencing

Copy and cut out along the dotted lines. Glue each story in order on another sheet of paper.

Left/Right

Below are several ideas for helping children learn the difference between left and right. This is a very difficult concept for young children. They will need many activities and lots of fun practice. Use the words left and right as you give directions or explain where things are located. The more often children hear the words, the more quickly they will learn to understand them.

A HANDY TRICK

Have the children hold up their left hands, palms facing outward. Show the children how to make an uppercase L by spreading their thumbs and pointer fingers. Explain that only the LEFT hand can form an L to help us remember which side is LEFT. Right hands cannot make an L.

LEFT AND RIGHT MITTENS

Make cut out mitten shapes. Have the children decorate the mittens and label them with an, "L" for LEFT and an "R" for RIGHT.

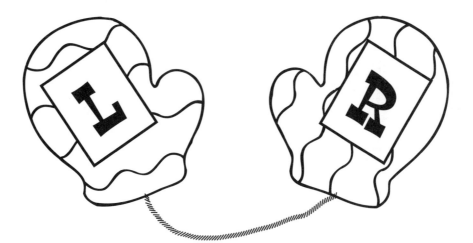

LEFT- AND RIGHT-HANDED BRACELETS

Photocopy the bracelet pattern below. Write an "L" in the blank if the child will be wearing it on the left wrist. Write an "R" if the child will be wearing it on the right wrist. Lengthen the sides as needed to fit the child's wrist properly.

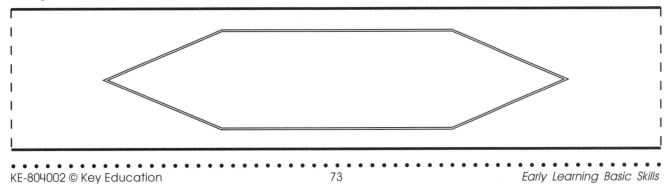

ABC • 123 • ABC • 123 • ABC • 123 • ABC • 123 • ABC • 123 • ABC • 123 • ABC • 123 • ABC

Top/Bottom Refrigerator Shelves

Copy, color, and cut out the pictures. Glue the things you drink on the **TOP** shelf. Glue the things you eat on the **BOTTOM** shelf.

Up and Down Climbing

Copy, color, and cut out the animals.
Glue the monkey climbing **UP** the tree.
Glue the lizard climbing **DOWN** the tree.

In and Out of Cages

Copy, color, and cut out the hamsters.
Glue one hamster **IN** the cage.
Glue the other hamster **OUT** of the cage.

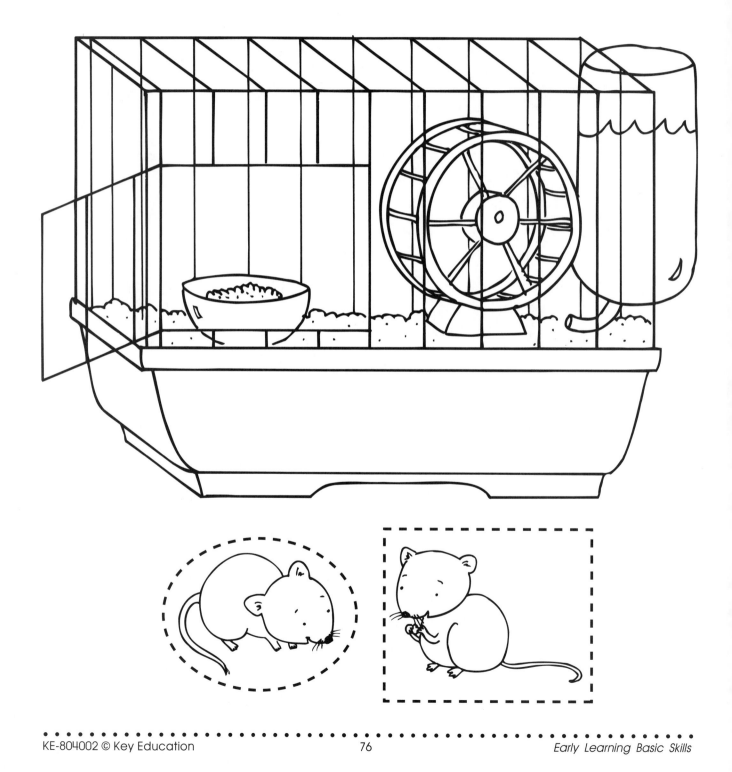

Many and Few

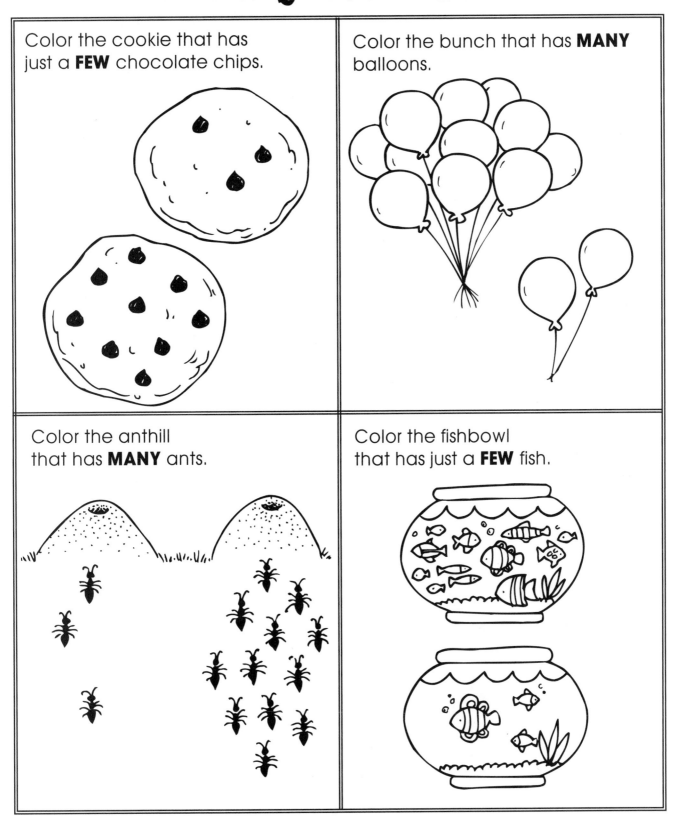

Color the cookie that has just a **FEW** chocolate chips.

Color the bunch that has **MANY** balloons.

Color the anthill that has **MANY** ants.

Color the fishbowl that has just a **FEW** fish.

Over and Under the Rainbow

Copy, color, and cut out the pot of gold and the birds.
Glue the pot of gold **UNDER** the rainbow.
Glue the birds **OVER** the rainbow.

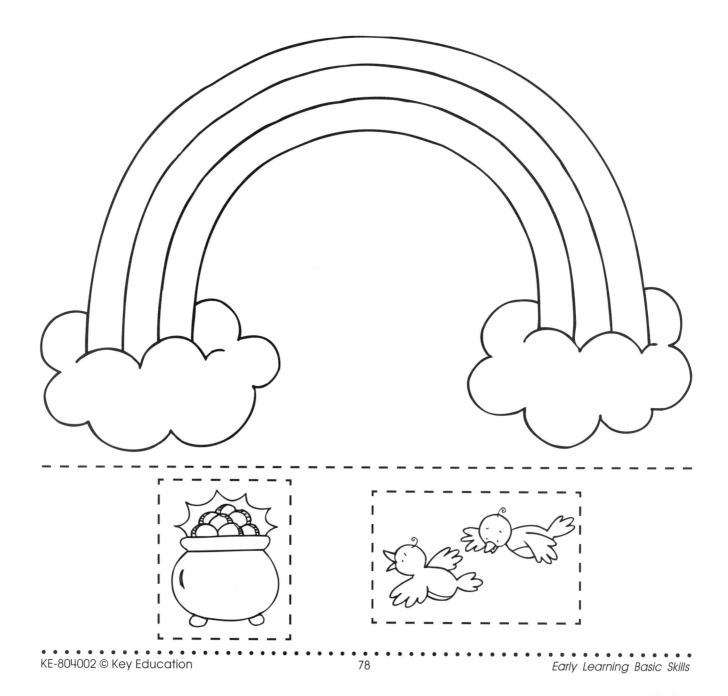

Who's Tall? Who's Short?

Copy, color, and cut out the ruler and the objects.
Measure each object. Put them in order from
tallest to shortest.

Real and Pretend

Color the **PRETEND** animals. Circle the **REAL** animals.

Letter "Aa"

Print.

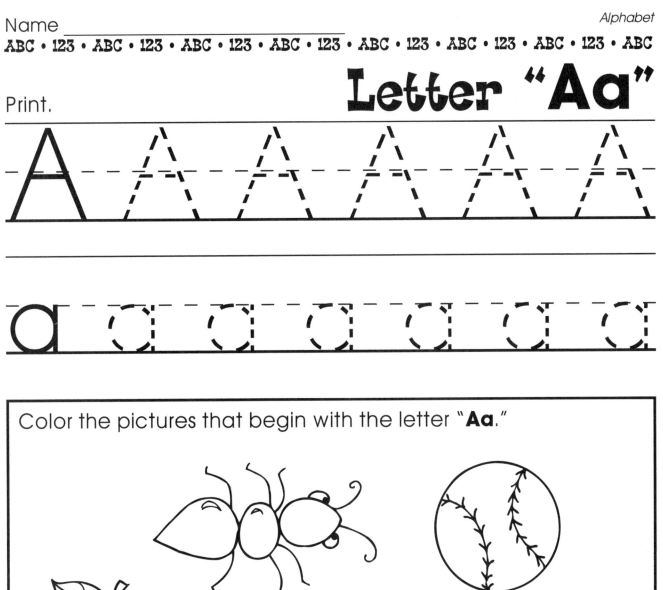

Color the pictures that begin with the letter "**Aa**."

Circle each uppercase **A** and lowercase **a**.

Letter "Bb"

Print.

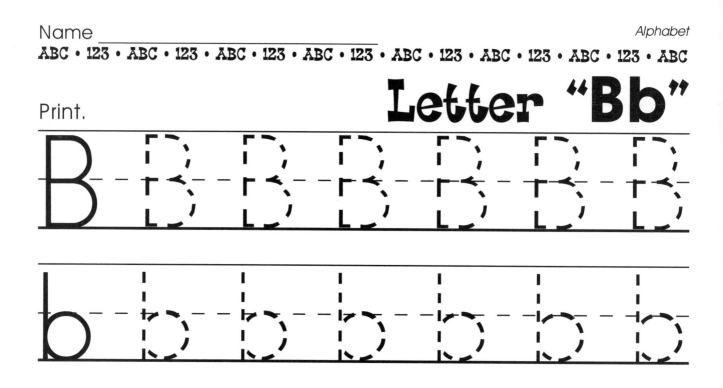

Color the pictures that begin with the letter "Bb."

Circle each uppercase **B** and lowercase **b.**

Find and color the things that start with "**Aa**."

Find and color the things that start with "**Bb**."

Print.

Letter "Cc"

Color the pictures that begin with the letter "**Cc**."

Circle each uppercase **C** and lowercase **c**.

Letter "Dd"

Print.

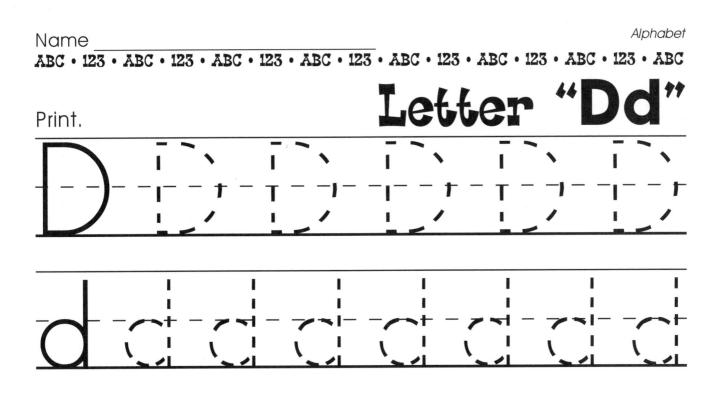

Color the pictures that begin with the letter "**Dd**."

Circle each uppercase **D** and lowercase **d**.

Name _____

Find and color the things that start with "**Cc**."

Find and color the things that start with "**Dd**."

Print.

Letter "Ee"

Color the pictures that begin with the letter "**Ee**."

Circle each uppercase **E** and lowercase **e**.

Letter "Ff"

Print.

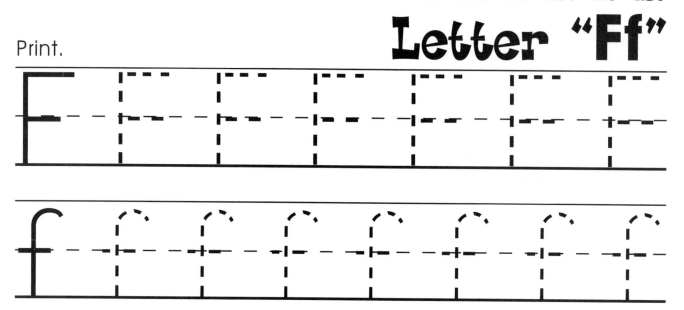

Color the pictures that begin with the letter "**Ff**."

Circle each uppercase **F** and lowercase **f**.

Find and color the things that start with "**Ee**."

Find and color the things that start with "**Ff**."

Letter "Gg"

Print.

Color the pictures that begin with the letter "**Gg**."

Circle each uppercase **G** and lowercase **g**.

p   G   P   g   a   G   g

g   b   G   G   g   Q   O   G

Letter "Hh"

Print.

Color the pictures that begin with the letter "**Hh**."

Circle each uppercase **H** and lowercase **h**.

Find and color the things that start with "**Gg**."

Find and color the things that start with "**Hh**."

Letter "Ii"

Print.

I I I I I I I I I I I I

i i i i i i i i i i i i

Color the pictures that begin with the letter "Ii."

Circle each uppercase **I** and lowercase **i**.

L I T I i L T

T i I i I i I

Letter "Jj"

Print.

Color the pictures that begin with the letter "**Jj**."

Circle each uppercase **J** and lowercase **j**.

j	J	d	P	q	J	p
i	j	J	J	l	j	j

Name _____

ABC • 123 • ABC • 123 • ABC • 123 • ABC • 123 • ABC • 123 • ABC • 123 • ABC • 123 • ABC

Find and color the things that start with "**Ii**."

- -

Find and color the things that start with "**Jj**."

Print.   # Letter "Kk"

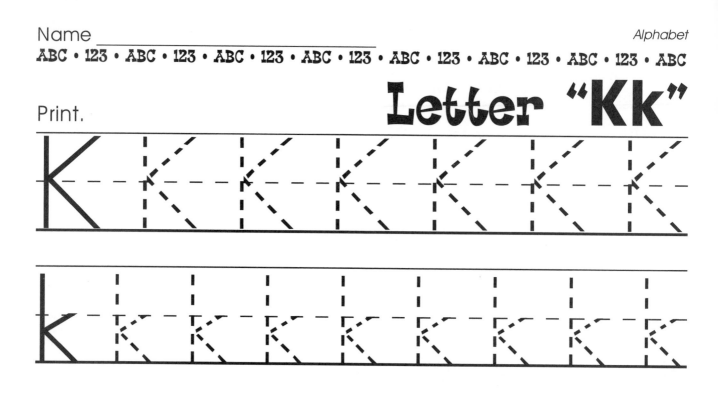

Color the pictures that begin with the letter "**Kk**."

Circle each uppercase **K** and lowercase **k**.

Letter "Ll"

Print.

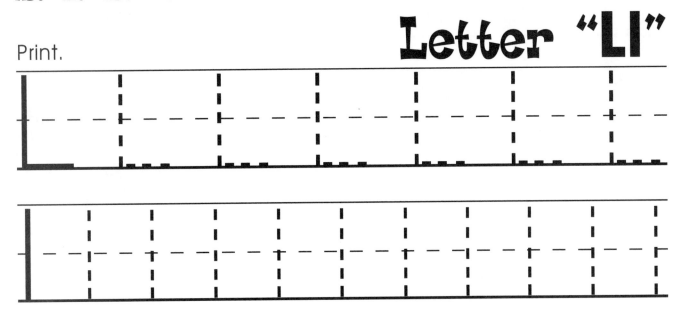

Color the pictures that begin with the letter "Ll."

Circle each uppercase **L** and lowercase **l**.

L	y	t	L	I	X	L
T	l	L	l	I	i	l

Find and color the things that start with "**Kk**."

Find and color the things that start with "**Ll**."

Print.

Letter "Mm"

M M M M M M M

m m m m m m m m

Color the pictures that begin with the letter "**Mm**."

Circle each uppercase **M** and lowercase **m**.

M **m** **X** **M** **M** **X** **m**

n **m** **M** **w** **N** **m** **n**

Print.

Letter "Nn"

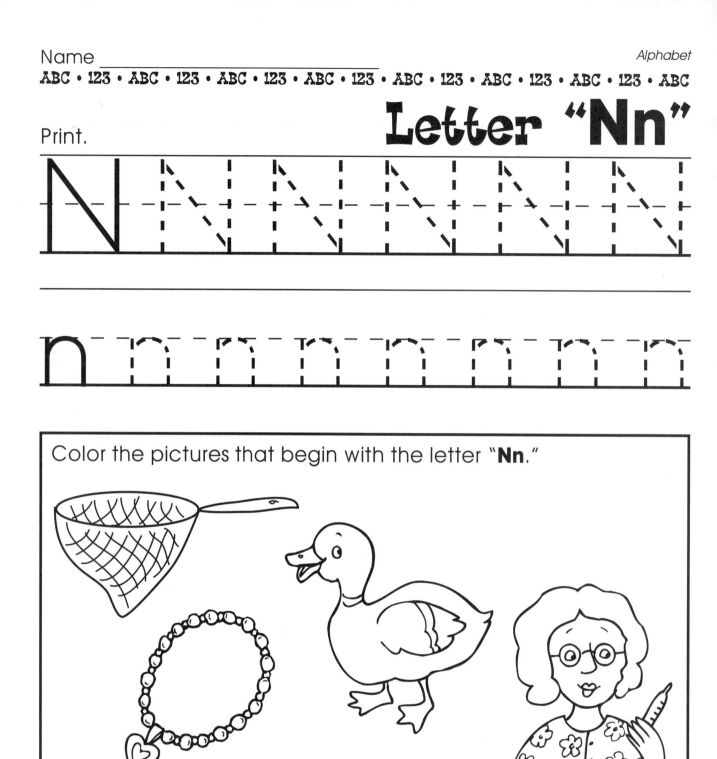

Color the pictures that begin with the letter "**Nn**."

Circle each uppercase **N** and lowercase **n**.

W m n V n M N

N n M N N n A

Find and color the things that start with "**Mm**."

Find and color the things that start with "**Nn**."

Letter "Oo"

Print.

Color the pictures that begin with the letter "**Oo**."

Circle each uppercase **O** and lowercase **o**.

Q	o	O	O	a	G	o
a	O	o	Q	O	o	q

Letter "Pp"

Print.

P P P P P P P

p p p p p p p

Color the pictures that begin with the letter "**Pp**."

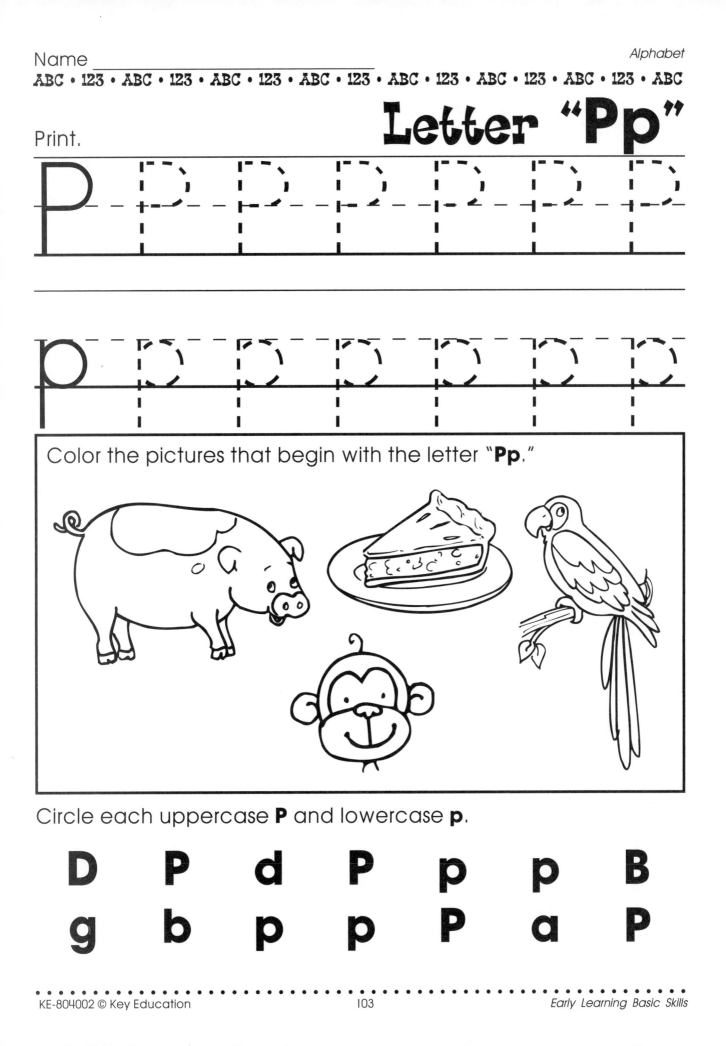

Circle each uppercase **P** and lowercase **p**.

D   P   d   P   p   p   B

g   b   p   p   P   a   P

Find and color the things that start with "**Oo**."

Find and color the things that start with "**Pp**."

Name _____
ABC • 123 • ABC • 123 • ABC • 123 • ABC • 123 • ABC • 123 • ABC • 123 • ABC • 123 • ABC

Alphabet

Letter "Qq"

Print.

Color the pictures that begin with the letter "**Qq**."

Circle each uppercase **Q** and lowercase **q**.

O Q q G a q G

q b Q D Q q Q

Print.

Letter "Rr"

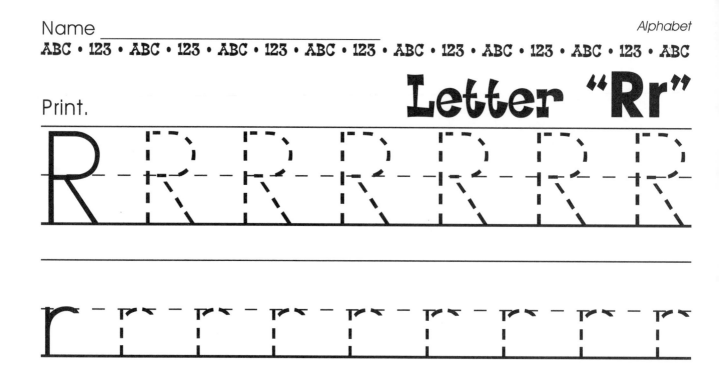

Color the pictures that begin with the letter "**Rr**."

Circle each uppercase **R** and lowercase **r**.

P   R   r   R   r   i   R
r   P   R   j   b   r   A

Find and color the things that start with "**Qq**."

Find and color the things that start with "**Rr**."

Print.

Letter "Ss"

S S S S S S S S

S S S S S S S S S S

Color the pictures that begin with the letter "**Ss**."

Circle each uppercase **S** and lowercase **s**.

Z   S   z   s   X   s   s

K   s   S   S   N   S   x

Letter "Tt"

Print.

T

t

Color the pictures that begin with the letter "Tt."

Circle each uppercase **T** and lowercase **t**.

ABC • 123 • ABC • 123 • ABC • 123 • ABC • 123 • ABC • 123 • ABC • 123 • ABC • 123 • ABC

Find and color the things that start with "**Ss**."

Find and color the things that start with "**Tt**."

Letter "Uu"

Print.

Color the pictures that begin with the letter "**Uu**."

Circle each uppercase **U** and lowercase **u**.

u	U	n	U	W	u	W
u	U	V	v	U	u	X

Print.

Letter "Vv"

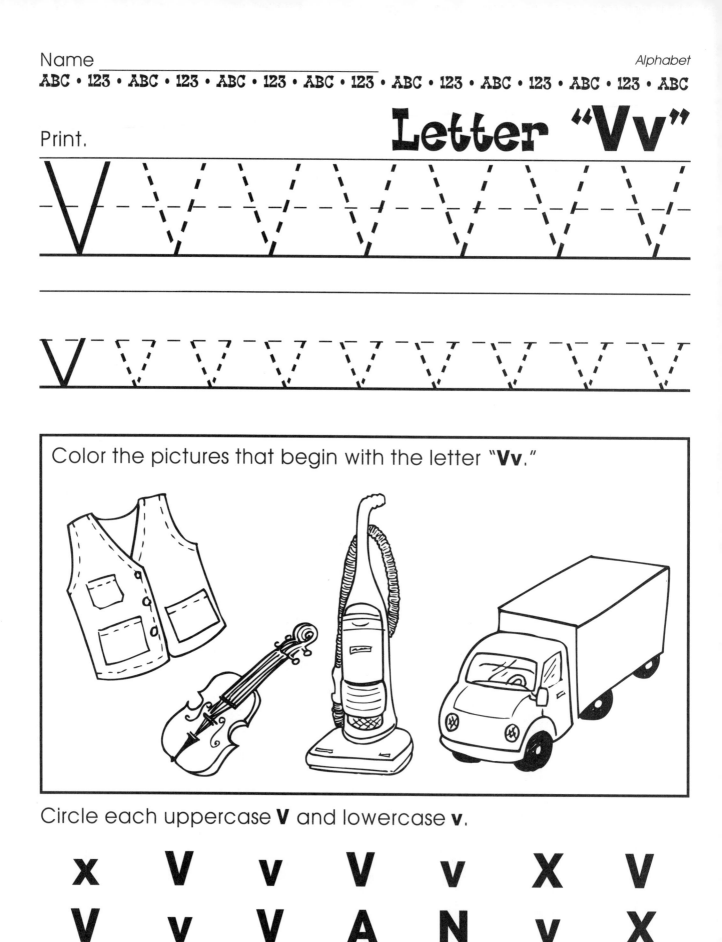

Color the pictures that begin with the letter "**Vv**."

Circle each uppercase **V** and lowercase **v**.

X V v V v X V

V v V A N v X

Find and color the things that start with "**Uu**."

Find and color the things that start with "**Vv**."

Print.

Letter "Ww"

Color the pictures that begin with the letter "**Ww**."

Circle each uppercase **W** and lowercase **w**.

Name _____

ABC • 123 • ABC • 123 • ABC • 123 • ABC • 123 • ABC • 123 • ABC • 123 • ABC • 123 • ABC

Letter "Xx"

Print.

Color the pictures that begin with the letter "**Xx**."

Circle each uppercase **X** and lowercase **x**.

K   **x**   **v**   **X**   **x**   **X**   **Z**

X   **v**   **x**   **A**   **X**   **N**   **x**

Find and color the things that start with "**Ww**."

Find and color things that contain the letter "**Xx**."

Name _____
ABC • 123 • ABC • 123 • ABC • 123 • ABC • 123 • ABC • 123 • ABC • 123 • ABC • 123 • ABC

Letter "Yy"

Print.

Color the pictures that begin with the letter "**Yy**."

Circle each uppercase **Y** and lowercase **y**.

y Y v V x Y Y

W y Y y N X y

Print.

Letter "Zz"

Color the pictures that begin with the letter "**Zz**."

Circle each uppercase **Z** and lowercase **z**.

H	Z	z	V	Z	X	W
z	Z	x	Z	V	z	z

ABC • 123 • ABC • 123 • ABC • 123 • ABC • 123 • ABC • 123 • ABC • 123 • ABC • 123 • ABC

Find and color the things that start with "**Yy**."

Find and color the things that start with "**Zz**."

An Alphabet Rhyming Book

A is for apple, so yummy to eat.

B is for bee, who makes honey so sweet.

C is for cat, who loves to purr.

D is for dog, with soft, fluffy fur.

E is for egg, with a chick inside.

F is for fish, who swims on his side.

G is for goat, who is wearing a hat.

H is for horse, who is carrying a rat.

I is for ink,
that comes
from a pen.

J is for jet,
flown by a hen.

K is for kite,
flying up
in the sky.

L is for lion,
who is eating
a pie.

M is for monkey,
who is funny
as can be.

N is for nest,
sitting high in
a tree.

O is for owl,
who plays music
all night.

P is for pig,
who is such
a muddy sight.

Q is for queen,
who wears
a gold crown.

R is for rabbit, who hops into town.

S is for seal, who slides on the ice.

T is for turtle, who is very nice.

U is for umbrella, that keeps off the rain.

V is for vulture, who is not tame.

W is for wagon, that is painted red.

X is for xylophone, that belongs to Ned.

Y is for yak, a very good friend.

Z is for zebra, who says, "This is the end."

ABC Order/Uppercase

Write the missing letters on the lines in alphabetical order.

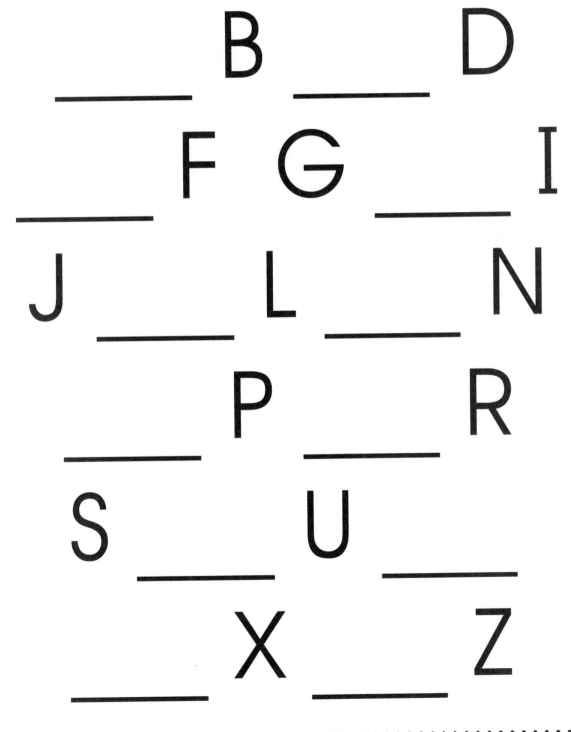

ABC Order/Lowercase

Write the missing letters on the lines in alphabetical order.

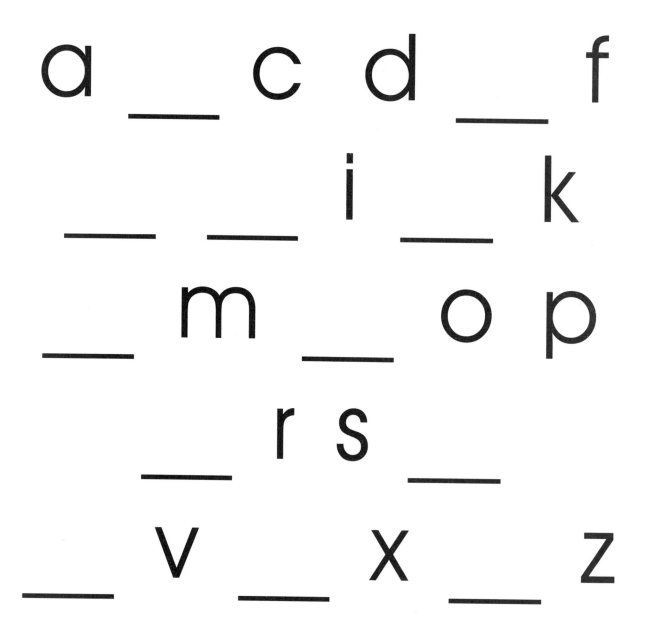

Uppercase ABC Dot-to-Dot

Connect the dots in alphabetical order.

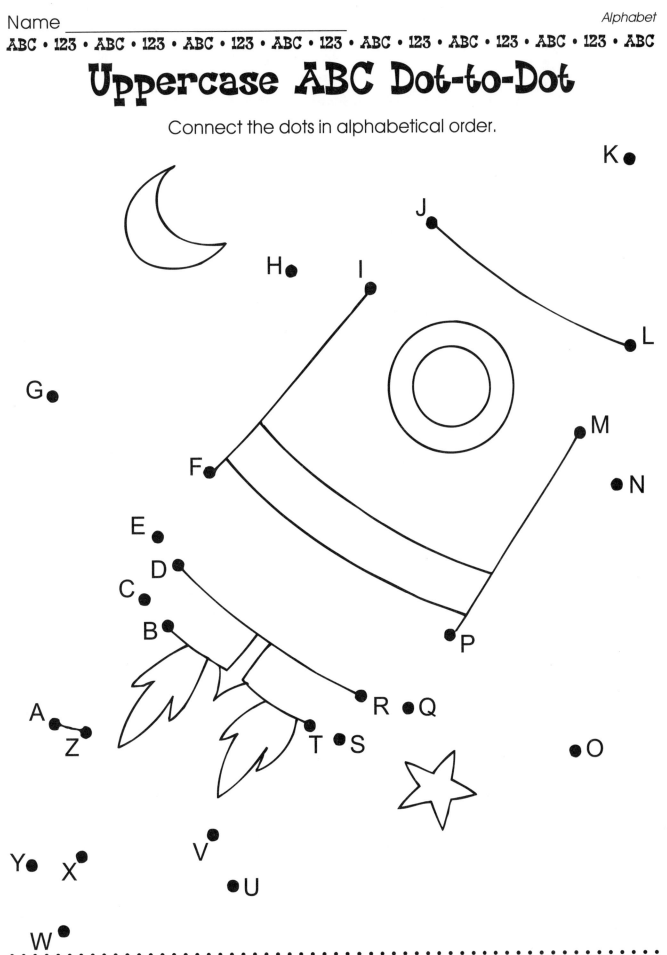

Lowercase ABC Dot-to-Dot

Connect the dots in alphabetical order.

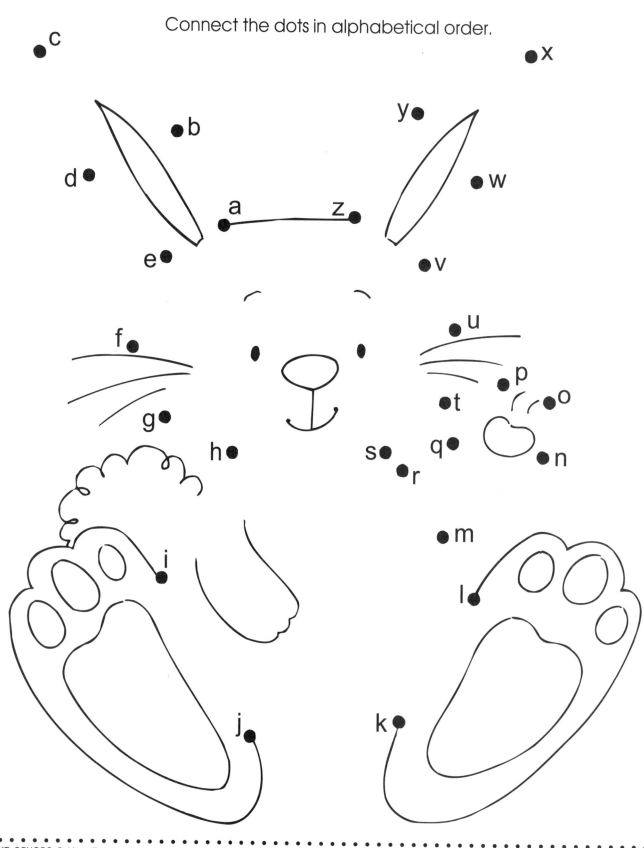

The sight word cards on pages 127–132 may be used in a variety of ways.

1. Make two copies of each word and let the children "match" words that are the same.
2. Play concentration.
3. Use as flash cards.
4. Use the cards to form simple sentences or phrases.

can

she

like

look

yes

he

it

me

no

see

is

Sight Words

and

all

cat

girl

big

the

at

boy

run

make

not

dog

Sight Words

up

this

want

who

that

come

will

we

down

jump

stop

you

Early Learning Basic Skills

be	have	said	go
for	do	little	get
has	good	ride	did

Sight Words

but	may	my	some
away	her	dad	there
are	him	mom	was

131

Early Learning Basic Skills

of

saw

been

your

were

on

when

way

does

off

play

then

Name _____

ABC • 123 • ABC • 123 • ABC • 123 • ABC • 123 • ABC • 123 • ABC • 123 • ABC • 123 • ABC

Zero "0"

Color **0**.

Trace.

O O O O O O O O O

zero zero zero

Connect the dots.

_____ candy in the jar.

One "1"

Color **1** puppy.

Trace.

1

one one one

Connect the dots.

Draw **1** cat.

Name _____

Two "2"

Color **2** kittens.

Trace.

2

two

Connect the dots.

Draw **2** balloons.

Early Learning Basic Skills

Three "3"

Color **3** ponies.

Trace.

3

three

Connect the dots.

Draw **3** cookies.

Name _____

Review 0 to 3

Circle the correct number.

Fill in the missing number.

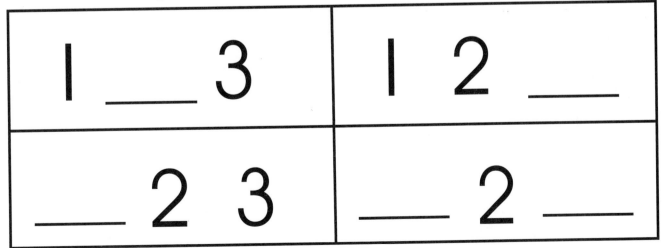

Four "4"

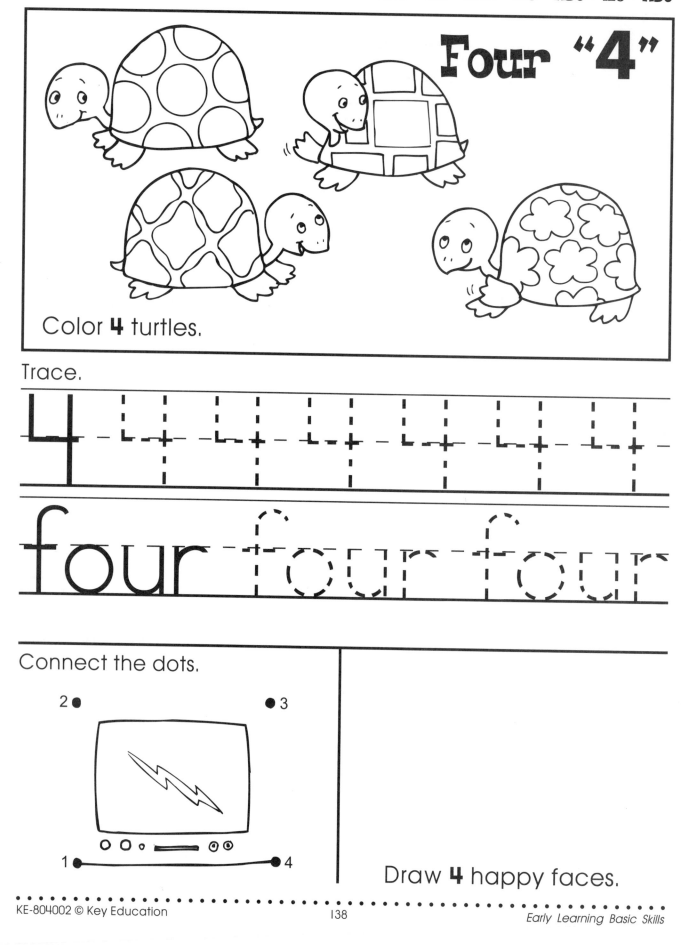

Color **4** turtles.

Trace.

4 -4- -4- -4- -4- -4- -4-

four four four

Connect the dots.

2 •   • 3

1 •   • 4

Draw **4** happy faces.

Five "5"

Color **5** birds.

Trace.

5 5 5 5 5 5 5

five five five

Connect the dots.

Draw **5** kites.

Six "6"

Color **6** bunnies.

Trace.

6 6 6 6 6 6

six six six six

Connect the dots.

Draw **6** balls.

Name _____

ABC • 123 • ABC • 123 • ABC • 123 • ABC • 123 • ABC • 123 • ABC • 123 • ABC • 123 • ABC

Color the correct number.   **Review 0 to 6**

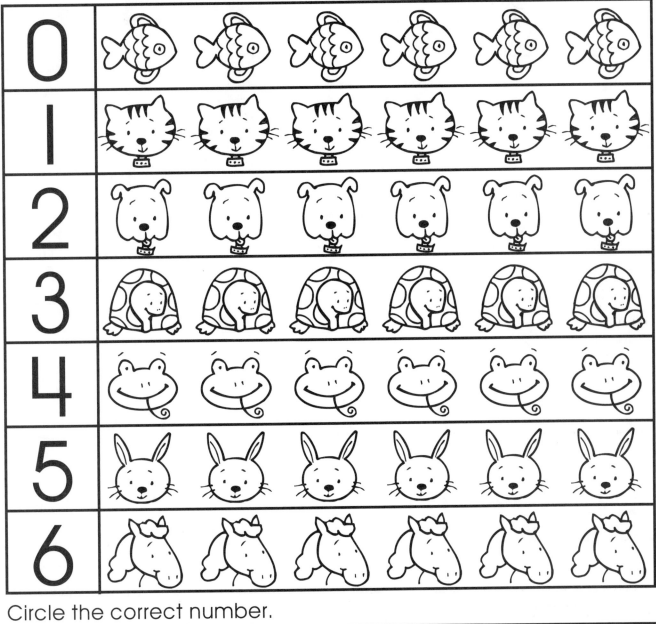

Circle the correct number.

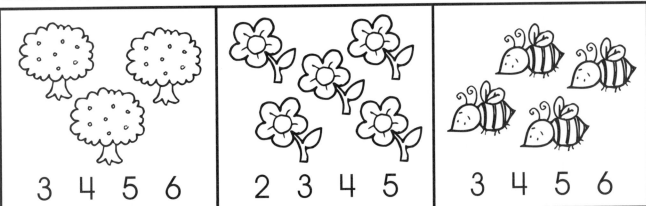

3   4   5   6   2   3   4   5   3   4   5   6

Seven "7"

Color **7** frogs.

Trace.

7 / / / / / / /

seven seven

Connect the dots.

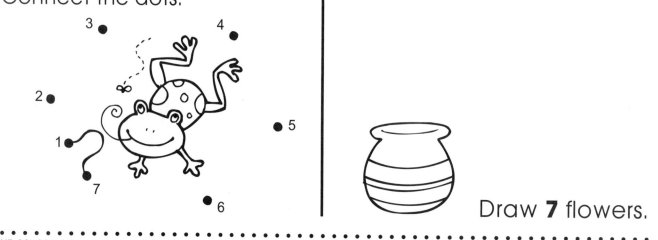

3 •
4 •
2 •
• 5
1
7 •
6 •

Draw **7** flowers.

Name _____

Eight "8"

Color **8** rockets.

Trace.

8

eight

Connect the dots.

STOP

4 5
3 6
2 7
1 8

Draw **8** stars.

Nine "9"

Color **9** ladybugs.

Trace.

q q q q q q q

nine nine nine

Connect the dots.

Draw **9** raindrops.

Review Zero to Nine

Read the number words and connect the dots in order.

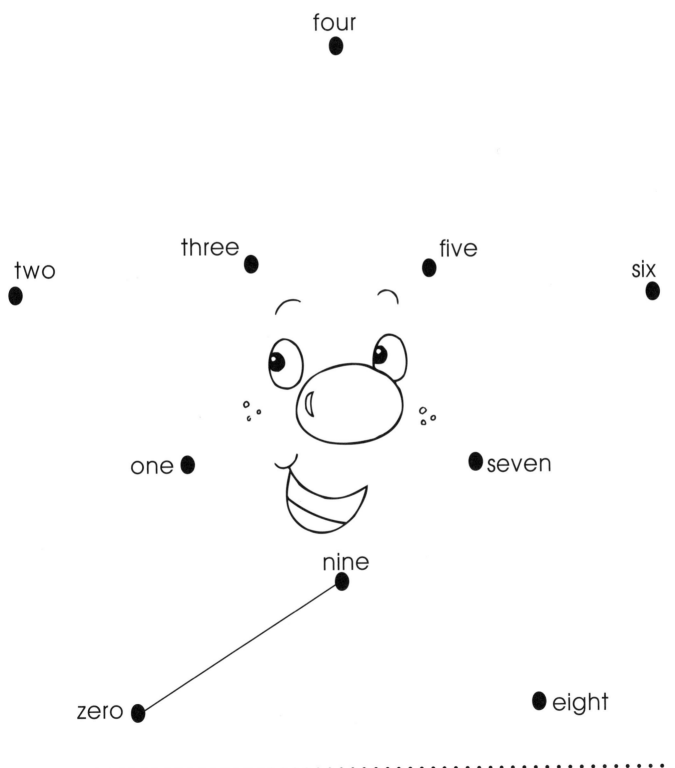

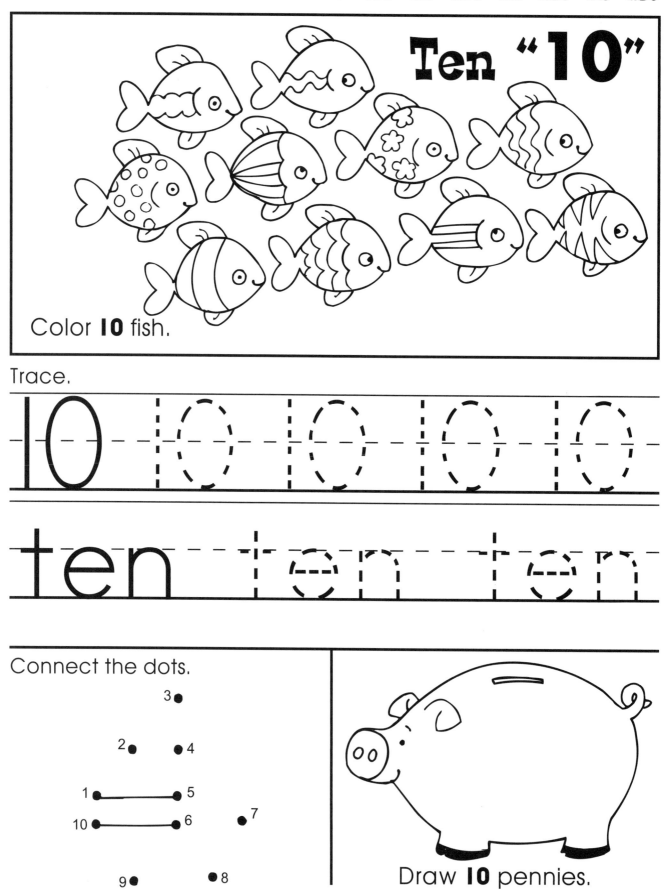

Ten "10"

Color **10** fish.

Trace.

10 10 10 10 10 10

ten ten ten

Connect the dots.

Draw **10** pennies.

Name _____

Eleven "11"

Color **11** bees.

Trace.

11

eleven eleven

Connect the dots.

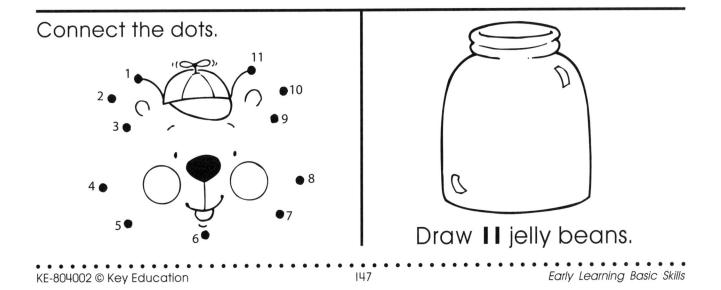

Draw **11** jelly beans.

Twelve "12"

Color **12** happy faces.

Trace.

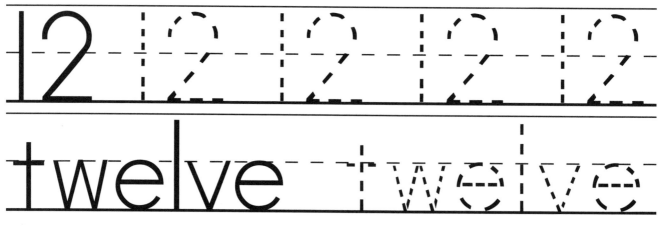

12 12 12 12 12

twelve twelve

Connect the dots.

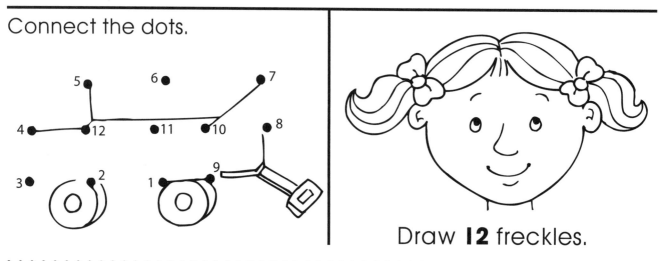

Draw **12** freckles.

Early Learning Basic Skills

Name _____

ABC • 123 • ABC • 123 • ABC • 123 • ABC • 123 • ABC • 123 • ABC • 123 • ABC • 123 • ABC

Review 1 to 12

Match the number word, to the numeral, and then to the set of objects. The first one is done for you.

six	1	◆◆◆◆
seven	2	❖❖❖❖❖
two	3	✳✳✳✳✳✳✳✳
one	4	▼
four	5	▲▲▲▲▲▲▲▲
three	6	▢▢
nine	7	❀❀❀❀❀
eleven	8	▢▢▢
five	9	✳✳✳✳✳✳✳✳✳
eight	10	▼▼▼▼▼▼▼
twelve	11	●●●●●●●●●●●●
ten	12	✳✳✳✳✳✳✳✳✳✳

Early Learning Basic Skills

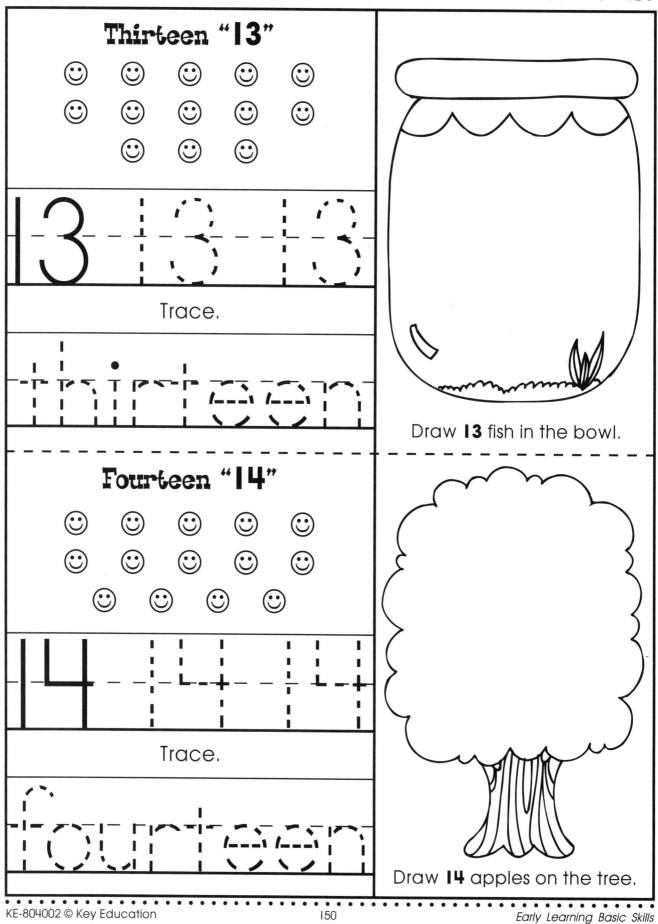

Thirteen "13"

13 13 13

Trace.

thirteen

Draw **13** fish in the bowl.

Fourteen "14"

14 14 14

Trace.

fourteen

Draw **14** apples on the tree.

Fifteen "15"

15 15 15

Trace.

fifteen

Draw **15** lollipops in the jar.

Sixteen "16"

16 16 16

Trace.

sixteen

Draw **16** buttons on the hat.

Edger Elephant

Connect the dots.

Review 1 to 16

Name ______________________________

ABC • 123 • ABC • 123 • ABC • 123 • ABC • 123 • ABC • 123 • ABC • 123 • ABC • 123 • ABC

Seventeen "17"

17 17 17

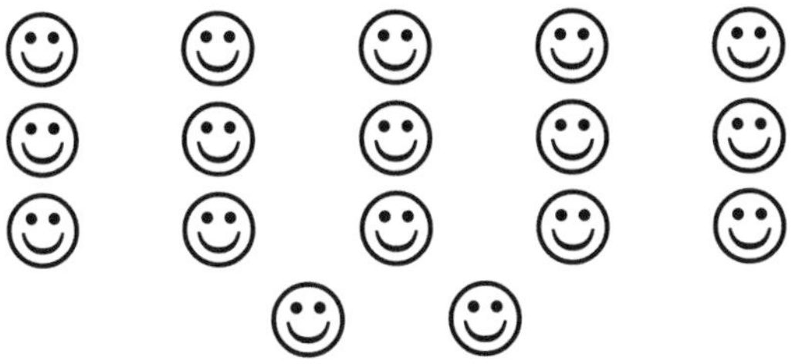

Trace.

seventeen

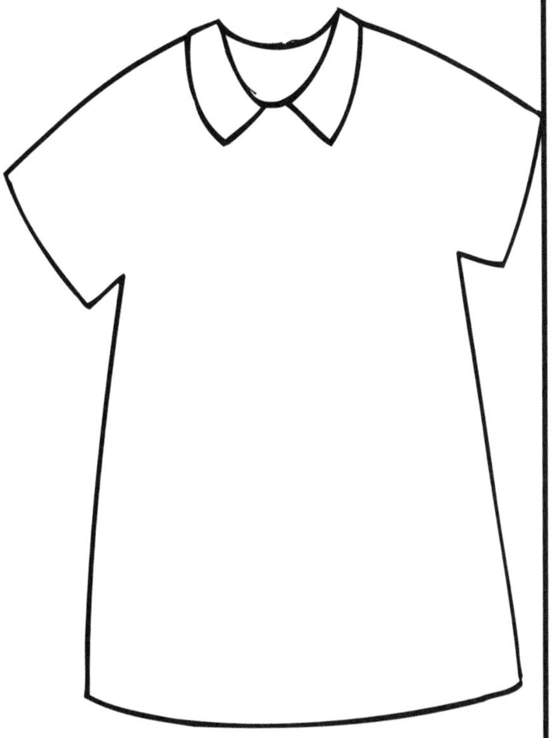

Draw **17** polka-dots on the shirt.

Eighteen "18"

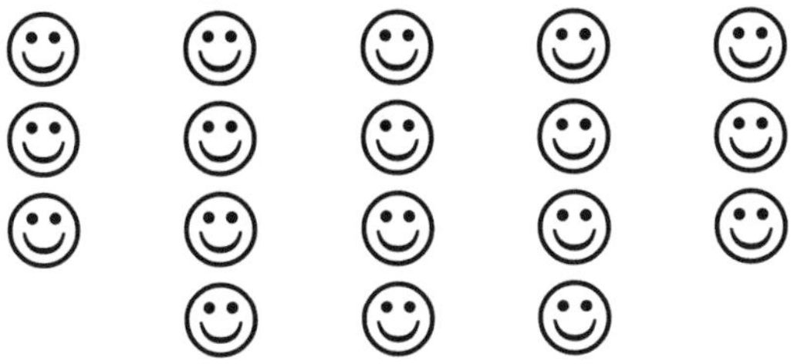

18 18 18

Trace.

eighteen

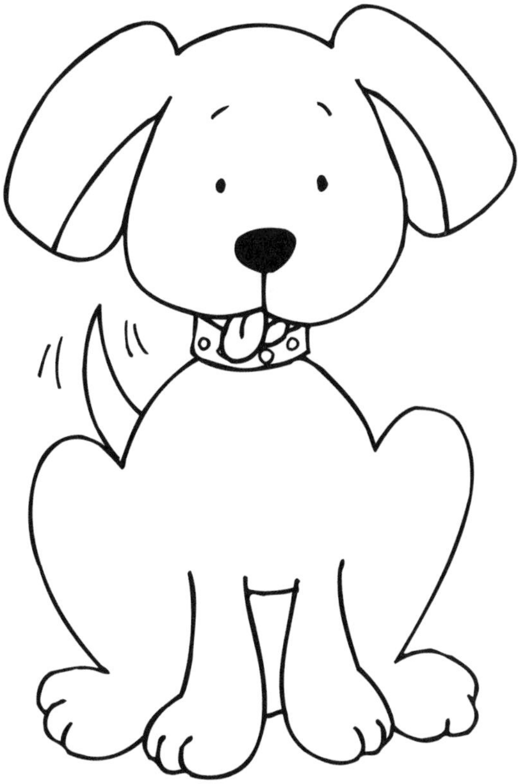

Draw **18** spots on the dog.

Nineteen "19"

19 19 19

Trace.

nineteen

Twenty "20"

20 20 20

Trace.

twenty

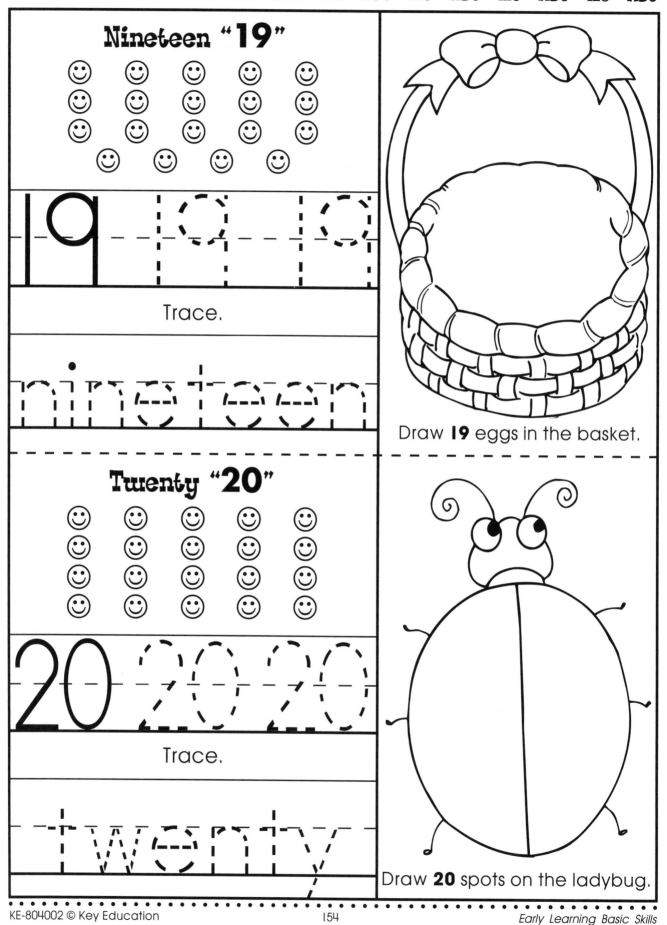

Draw **19** eggs in the basket.

Draw **20** spots on the ladybug.

Review 1 to 20

Fill in the missing numbers.

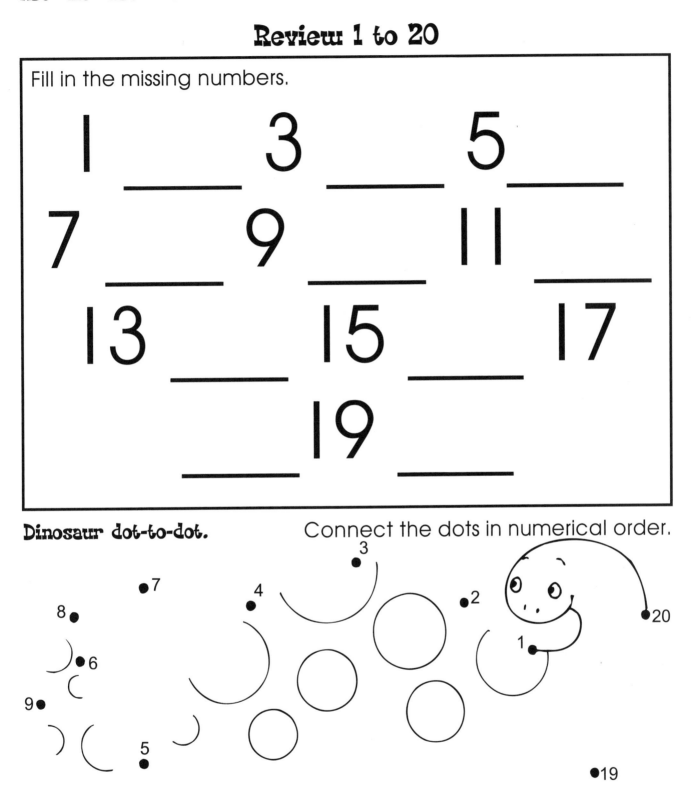

1   ___   3   ___   5   ___

7   ___   9   ___   11   ___

13   ___   15   ___   17

___   19   ___   ___

Dinosaur dot-to-dot.   Connect the dots in numerical order.

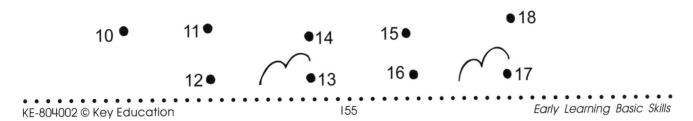

Fill in the missing numbers.   ## Counting 1 to 30

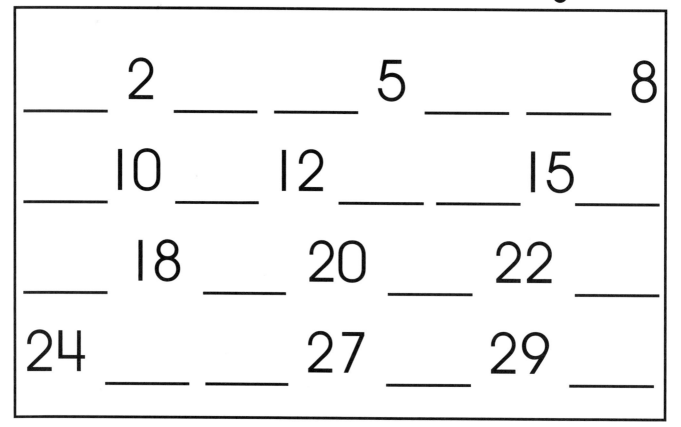

___ 2 ___ ___ 5 ___ ___ 8

___ 10 ___ 12 ___ ___ 15 ___

___ 18 ___ 20 ___ 22 ___

24 ___ ___ 27 ___ 29 ___

Follow the Maze!   Connect the dots 1 to 30

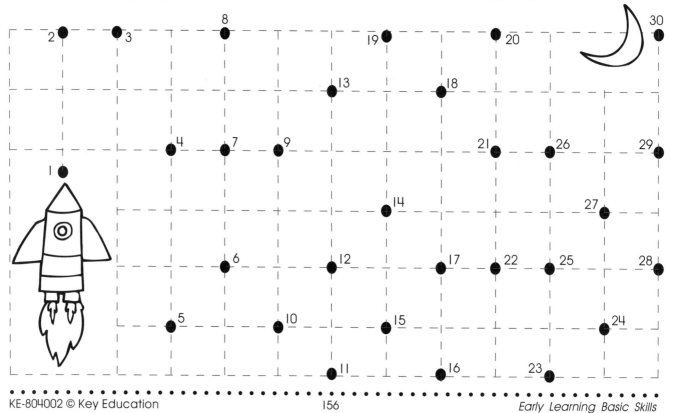

Name _____

ABC • 123 • ABC • 123 • ABC • 123 • ABC • 123 • ABC • 123 • ABC • 123 • ABC • 123 • ABC

Number Line from 0 to 30

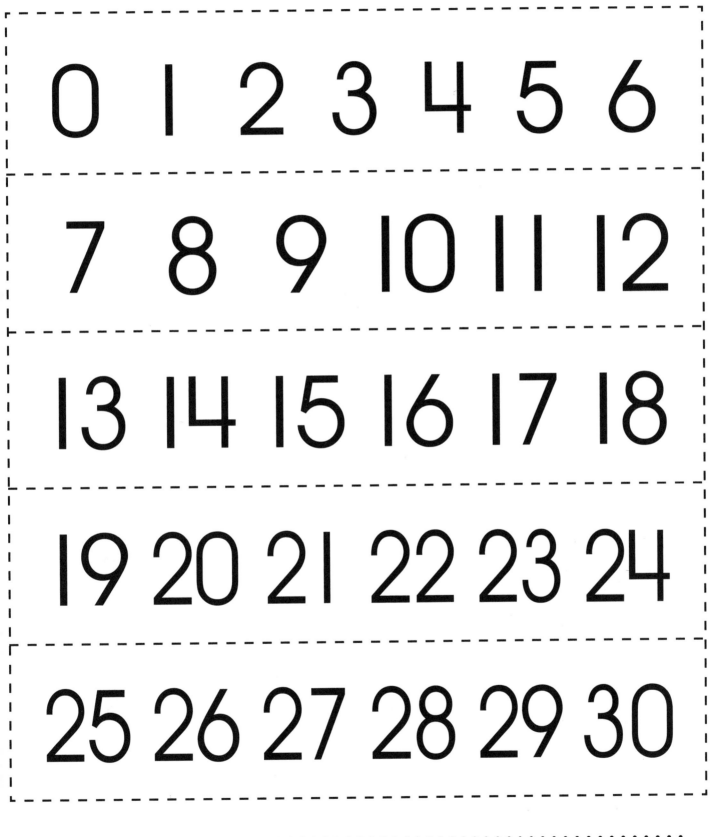

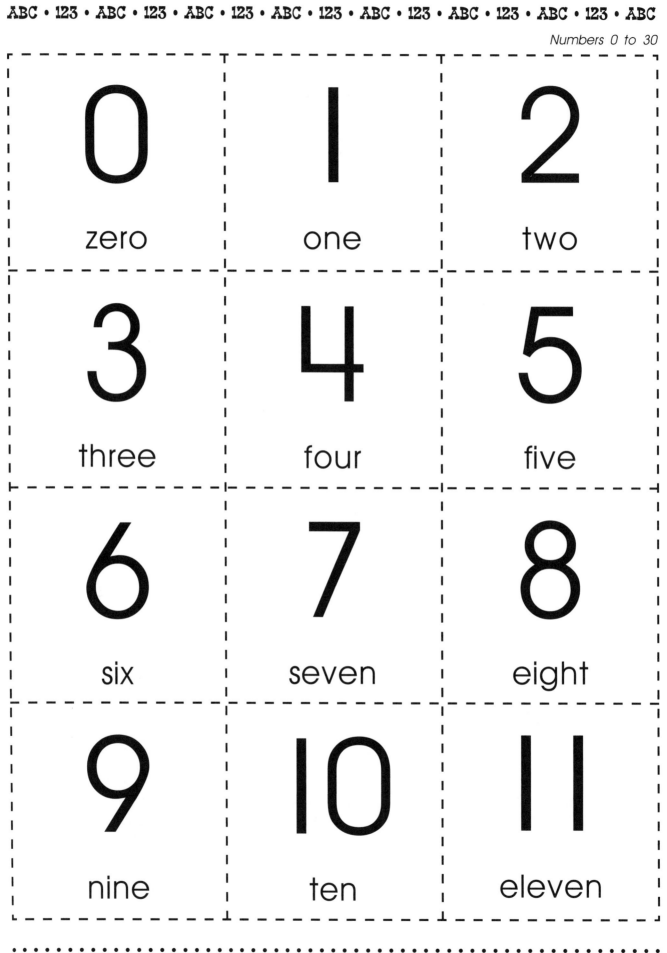

0
zero

1
one

2
two

3
three

4
four

5
five

6
six

7
seven

8
eight

9
nine

10
ten

11
eleven

12	13	14
twelve	thirteen	fourteen
15	16	17
fifteen	sixteen	seventeen
18	19	20
eighteen	nineteen	twenty
21	22	23
twenty-one	twenty-two	twenty-three

24
twenty-four

25
twenty-five

26
twenty-six

27
twenty-seven

28
twenty-eight

29
twenty-nine

30
thirty

+

−

=

Activities with Flash Cards
- Put the number cards in order from smallest to the greatest.
- Use the cards to count by 2s, 3s, and 5s.
- Make addition and subtraction problems using the number cards and the operational symbols.
- Draw the correct number of dots on the back of each card.
- Play the card game "War." Photocopy several sets of the number cards. Divide the cards equally among the children. Have the children turn over one card at a time. The child with the greatest number wins all of the cards.